Greek Endgame

Greek Endgame

From Austerity to Growth or Grexit

Nicos Christodoulakis

ROWMAN & LITTLEFIELD
INTERNATIONAL

London • New York

Published by Rowman & Littlefield International, Ltd.
Unit A, Whitacre Mews, 26-34 Stannary Street, London SE11 4AB
www.rowmaninternational.com

Rowman & Littlefield International, Ltd. is an affiliate of Rowman & Littlefield
4501 Forbes Boulevard, Suite 200, Lanham, Maryland 20706, USA
With additional offices in Boulder, New York, Toronto (Canada), and Plymouth (UK)
www.rowman.com

British Library Cataloguing in Publication Data
A catalogue record for this book is available from the British Library

ISBN: HB 978-1-78348-523-9
       PB 978-1-78348-524-6

Library of Congress Cataloging-in-Publication Data
Christodoulakis, N. M. (Nicos M.), author.
Greek endgame : from austerity to growth or Grexit / Nicos Christodoulakis.
   pages cm
ISBN 978-1-78348-523-9 (cloth : alk. paper) — ISBN 978-1-78348-524-6
(pbk. : alk. paper) — ISBN 978-1-78348-525-3 (electronic)
1. Debts, External—Greece. 2. Debts, Public—Greece. 3. Financial crises—Greece.
4. Greece—Economic policy—1974–5. Greece—Economic conditions—1974–6.
European Union—Greece. I. Title.
HJ8673.C47 2015
330.9495—dc23

                                                                    2015025863

Printed in the United States of America

Contents

List of Illustrations

FIGURES

TABLES

Glossary

ARS	The currency code for Argentinean Peso; the symbol is $.
BPS	The currency code for British Pound Sterling
CPI	Consumer Price Index
EC	European Commission
ECB	European Central Bank
EEC	European Economic Community
EFSF	European Financial Stability Facility
EMU	Economic and Monetary Union
Entry parity	The exchange rate of joining the euro, set at 340.5 drachma/€.
ERM	Exchange Rate Mechanism
ESM	European Stability Mechanism
EU	European Union
Euribor	Euro Interbank Offered Rate
Eurogroup	Council of Finance Ministers of the Eurozone countries
Eurostat	European Statistical Service
FDI	Foreign Direct Investment
Forex	Foreign exchange market
FYROM	Former Yugoslav Republic of Macedonia
GDP	Gross Domestic Product
GES	Gold Exchange Standard
Haircut	Debt reduction by cutting the nominal value of issued bonds
HFSF	Hellenic Financial Stability Fund (ΤΧΣ)
HRADF	Hellenic Republic Asset Development Fund (ΤΑΙΠΕΔ)
IMF	International Monetary Fund
IPO	Initial Public Offering
MEFP	Memorandum of Economic and Financial Policies

Memorandum	The programme of Specific Economic Policy Conditionality
MFAFA	Master Financial Assistance Facility Agreement
OMT	Open Market Transactions
OSI	Official Sector Involvement
PSI	Private Sector Involvement
PUC	Public Utility Corporation (ΔΕΚΟ)
QE	Quantitative Easing (by the Central Bank)
Troika	The representatives of IMF, European Central Bank and the Eurogroup
ULC	Unit Labour Cost
USD	The currency code for US Dollar
VAT	Value Added Tax (ΦΠΑ)
WEO	World Economic Outlook, IMF publication

Calendar of Main
Crisis-Related Events

August 2007: A snap election is called by the incumbent New Democracy Party (centre-right) on the grounds that public finances are getting out of control and a new consolidation policy is needed. Shortly after the announcement in mid-August, devastating wildfires claim dozens of human lives and cause extensive environmental damage. The government pledges compensations and a relief fund is set up.

September 2007: Elections are won by the incumbent government, albeit its majority is slashed. No special measures are taken.

January 2008: The international credit environment deteriorates, but the government announces that the Greek economy is sufficiently fortressed against external shocks. Emergency fiscal measures are ruled out.

September 2008: The global economic crisis erupts, but Greece does not suffer any serious recession at first. Greek banks are capitalized by €5 billion. The government says that this is only a precautionary measure.

December 2008: Serious riots in Athens and other cities in Greece after a youth is shot dead by police. Clashes last for two weeks and are extensively covered by world media; several of them mistook the events as being a reaction to the crisis and interpreted them as a prelude to similar protests elsewhere. A government reshuffle in January 2009 includes the Ministry of Finance.

May 2009: In the European elections, the incumbent party loses by landslide and soon opts for yet another snap general election, just two years after the previous one. Economic policy is virtually abandoned and public deficit gets out of control. Wildfires occur again in the summer.

October 2009: The socialist party wins the elections by landslide, and, immediately afterwards, the government announces that the public deficit is running above 11% of GDP versus an initial target of 3.7%. The figure is later finalized at 15.4% of GDP.

December 2009: The 2010 Government Budget Plan endorses several pre-electoral promises. Rating agencies Fitch, Moody's and Standard & Poor serially downgrade Greece, but the government remains hesitant in coping with the looming crisis.

January 2010: After taking part in the World Economic Forum at Davos, Switzerland, the Greek government talks increasingly in favour of inviting IMF to Greece. Spreads on Greek bonds are rising, but the government insists on issuing bonds with long maturities instead of short-term ones, whose costs remain low, thanks to the ECB liquidity facilities.

April–May 2010: Greece seeks a bailout. Following the request, a joint IMF/Eurozone/ECB mission visits Greece and the First Memorandum of Economic and Financial Policies is signed. A financing package of €110 billion is disbursed. Clashes erupt in Athens and three people are killed when demonstrators attack a small private bank.

June 2011: The Memorandum is extended by the medium-term fiscal-adjustment strategy. It aims at primary surpluses and privatizations of up to €50 billion to control the dynamics of debt.

September 2011: The government breaks talks with Troika members. To return, they demand the introduction of a special property levy payable together with the electricity bill. Wide protests follow and many refuse to pay.

February 2012: The Second Memorandum of Economic and Financial Policies is ratified by Greek Parliament amid serious clashes in Athens and party splits. The programme provides for financial assistance of €164.5 billion until the end of 2014.

March 2012: The debt reduction ('haircut') is completed. Greek banks are recapitalized through the Greek Financial Stability Fund, which becomes the major shareholder, while the capital injection is recorded on the Greek public debt.

May–June 2012: Two successive general elections are held after the first fails to produce a governing majority. In June, a coalition government is formed by the conservative, socialist and Democratic Left parties. The left-wing opposition rises; the far-right party ('Golden Dawn') is elected to Parliament.

December 2012: The Memorandum is amended. Its main aim is to overhaul the tax system and introduce a new property tax.

June–September 2013: The government shuts down the National Television and the Democratic Left party leaves the coalition. Following the murder of an activist, the leadership of the far-right party is arrested on conspiracy charges.

April 2014: Four years after the bailout, Greece holds its first government bond auction. Part of the primary surplus is distributed to selected public sector groups, mainly the police and armed forces personnel. The property tax is introduced to replace the special property levy. The government is heavily criticized for mistakes and excessiveness.

May 2014: In the European elections, the Radical Left coalition (Syriza) comes on top. The far-right party gets nearly 10% of the vote.

September 2014: The coalition government pledges that it is about to complete the programme and tap the markets. Meetings with the Troika are not productive and new austerity measures are demanded. Debt sustainability is in doubt and proposals for rescheduling and/or reduction appear. Wide protests on the property tax force the government to allow payments in instalments.

December 2014: Second Amendment of the Second Memorandum. The government asks for a two-month extension and access to the precautionary credit line facility by the ESM. An early presidential election (normally due in May 2015) is inconclusive and new general elections are announced. Talks with creditors stall.

January 2015: The Syriza party wins the general election with the mandate to abolish the Memorandum and keep the country in the Eurozone. A coalition government is formed with the Eurosceptic nationalist party of 'Independent Greeks'. Amid protracted negotiations between Greece and the Euro group, Grexit is viewed as increasingly likely.

Prologue

The dilemma of a Greek exit from the Eurozone (Grexit) acquired a new momentum both in Greece and abroad after the Radical Left coalition (*Syriza*) won the January 2015 general election and formed a government with a Eurosceptic nationalist party. Even though before the elections the party had pledged its unequivocal endorsement of the euro, the government has since sought to relax the existing policy mix, and this led to protracted disagreements and negotiations with the European lenders and the IMF. It was only a matter of time before the Grexit scenario returned full-scale to the fore, to be discussed as the likely outcome of Greece's failure to reach a new agreement. At the time of completing this book, the debate was fervent and all options were open. Domestic public opinion appeared to be in favour of keeping the common currency, but several analysts openly suggested that the political and economic obstacles lying ahead were insurmountable and would eventually lead to the unthinkable. At the same time, several international commentators—through a frenzy of media coverage—either openly supported or, at least, entertained the idea of a return to the historical currency of the drachma.

For all these reasons, it is imperative to rekindle the debate regarding the comparative advantages of the euro and the drachma for the country. First and foremost, to separate the effects of economic policy implemented in Greece from the constraints actually imposed by the single currency; second, to demonstrate that the euro remains by far the most beneficial option for Greece, as compared to an unstable and deeply devalued currency that may replace it. Escaping from the current recession and unemployment requires the implementation of another policy mix within the Eurozone, and not another currency by leaving it.

* * *

This volume is based on books that I have published in Greece and on my numerous research articles published in international journals, plus new material and policy assessment. The links between current text and previous work is delineated in the Appendix.

Unavoidably, in a book focusing on a situation that potentially may change rapidly as current affairs and political vicissitudes in Greece are still unfolding, there are aspects that may be superseded by events during the process of its preparation. As the purpose of this work is to give the reader a clear background to the current economic situation in Greece and to provide the justification for certain approaches to tackling the problem, it is hoped that any such events may render the work useful in terms of anticipating what might happen with certain policy decisions or could have been avoided with others.

The book contains many economic facts that some readers may find tedious or abstruse. However, they are indispensable because this is exactly what differentiates this text from other descriptions, which gloss over these facts. In order to provide for easier reading, economic tables and charts have been set apart from the main text, while all notes appear as endnotes. Although the analysis is based on the best available statistical data, responsibility for processing and evaluating them lies solely with the author.

In preparing the book, I have greatly benefited from the comments and suggestions by two anonymous referees on an earlier plan of the book, and the continuous support and help by Alison Howson. I am deeply thankful to Nicos Roussos for translating substantial parts from two books that I had published in Greek, and also to Anastasia Tsadaris for editorial assistance. Naturally, I remain solely responsible for any errors and omissions that may still exist in the text.

N.C.
Athens, May 2015

Introduction

THE SPECTRE OF GREXIT

In May 2010 and after months of credit shortages and looming repayments of public debt, Greece finally sought a bailout agreement with the European Union (EU), International Monetary Fund (IMF) and European Central Bank (ECB), henceforth code named as 'Troika'. In return for the bailout funds, Greece accepted the *Memorandum of Understanding on Specific Economic Policy Conditionality* (the Memorandum), a blueprint with specific policies to be implemented in order to reduce indebtedness and promote growth. Things, however, did not go as smoothly as planned nor as initially expected.

The Unforeseen Transformation of Greece

The dogged implementation of austerity programmes in Greece in exchange for the bailout in May 2010 has brought about tectonic shifts, not only in the economy but also in the political structures and social dynamics, even in the geopolitical perception of the country on the global stage. Table 0.1 demonstrates the outcome of the national and European elections held in Greece since 2007. The two mainstream parties that were alternating in power since the restoration of democracy in 1974 saw their influence dither away from around 80% of the vote to little more than 30%. Their ex-supporters either followed splinter groups or voted *en masse* for the Radical Left coalition (Syriza) that was catapulted from just 5% of the vote in 2007 to over 36% in 2015, forming a government with radical left-wing leanings for the first time in Greek history. An ominous outcome was the electoral consolidation of 'Golden Dawn', the far-right party that managed to rise from non-existence to the third position in the Greek Parliament.

Table 0.1   Election Results in Greece 2007–2015

Political Party	N2007 Sep	E2009 May	N2009 Oct	N2012 May	N2012 Jun	E2014 May	N2015 Jan
ND (centre-right)	41.84%	32.30%	33.47%	18.85%	29.66%	22.72%	27.81%
Pasok (centre-left)	38.10%	36.65%	43.92%	13.18%	12.28%	8.02%	4.68%
KKE (communist)	8.15%	8.35%	7.54%	8.48%	4.50%	6.11%	5.47%
Syriza (radical left)	5.04%	4.70%	4.60%	16.79%	26.89%	26.56%	36.34%
Laos (rightwing)	3.80%	7.15%	5.63%	2.89%	1.58%	2.69%	1.03%
XA (far right)	0.03%	0.46%	0.29%	6.97%	6.92%	9.39%	6.28%
Splinter/new							
Anel (ND & Laos)				10.62%	7.51%	3.46%	4.75%
Demar (from Syriza)				6.11%	6.25%	1.20%	0.49%
Potami (Pasok & Demar)						6.61%	6.05%
Drasi—Xana (from ND)		0.76 %		3.95%	1.59%	0.91%	
Kidiso (from Pasok)							2.46%

National (N) and European elections (E). *Source*: Ministry for the Interior, Greece.

Party acronyms: ND (New Democracy); Pasok (Panhellenic Socialist Movement); KKE (Communist Party of Greece); Syriza (Coalition of Radical Left); Laos (People's Orthodox Alert); XA (Golden Dawn); Anel (Independent Greeks); Demar (Democratic Left); Potami (River); Drasi—Xana (Action—Construction Again); Kidiso (Movement of Democratic Socialism).

Note: The origins of splinter parties are attributed by the author.

The background of these developments is the deep economic downturn. The end result of the austerity programme has been the largest depression experienced by any other European country during the twentieth century in non-war years. One of the consequences of the adjustment failure has been the emergence of a potential *Grexit,* that is to say Greece exiting the common currency, defaulting on its debt and re-establishing competitiveness by a drastic devaluation of its currency.

Very few people were concerned about such potential ramifications at the beginning. The policies that began to be implemented under the aegis of the Troika aimed at dealing with a huge fiscal and a large external deficit, in order to control the ballooning debt and enable the country's swift return to international markets. The implementation horizon was brief and benefits were expected to be evident quickly, whereas any adverse consequences would be limited and temporary.

When the first stage of the adjustment programme failed, the policy was neither revised nor was the intensity of its implementation called into question. Instead, amidst a pandemonium of political bickering and social unrest, the first programme was replaced by a second one in 2011, which also proved insufficient to get the country out of the crisis. The new measures were identical to those of the first stage in terms of character, style and outcome: namely, across-the-board wage cuts, a new wave of taxes, an abysmal failure to privatize public assets and a systematic aversion for any real change in the public sector.

Apart from other reasons, the key factor was that, despite the fiscal adjustment, the economy did not come out of recession nor was the debt burden harnessed. On the contrary, the economy, after contracting by a further –4% in 2013, barely changed in 2014 and showed no sign of a systematic return to growth. As depicted in Figure 0.1, Greece suffered from a recession that was much harder than that experienced by the other economies of Eurozone's periphery during their own austerity programmes.

Some Success, Too Late

Success came late but was still limited in scope and far from being robust. Most importantly, the performance of the Greek economy in 2014 checked somewhat Europe's censure of Greece as a country in permanent failure (see Figure 0.2). Based on the latest data for 2014, Greece is no longer the worst fiscal performer in the Eurozone: government deficit fell at 3.5% of GDP,

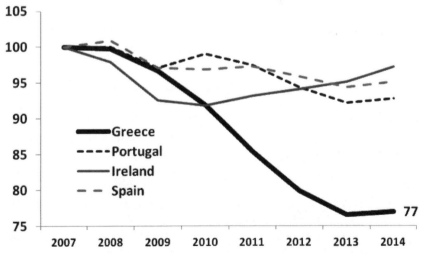

Figure 0.1 Real GDP Index, Base 2007=100. *Source*: AMECO Eurostat, rebased. (Figures for 2014 are estimates).

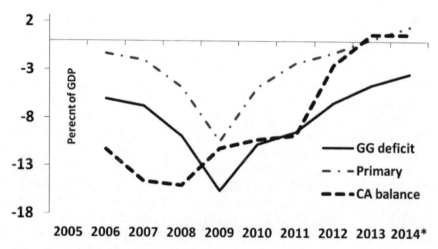

Figure 0.2 Public and External Balances.

more than half of its level of two years before and lower than that of five other Eurozone members. It was also substantially lower than the deficits of the United Kingdom and the United States and about a third of the deficit of Japan in that year; −5.7%, −4.9% and −7.8% of GDP, respectively. The primary deficit turned also into a surplus (0.4% of GDP), higher than that of eleven other Eurozone countries.[1] If balances are cyclically adjusted, that is, calculated by taking into account the extent of recession, Greece emerges as the 2014 fiscal champion by achieving a primary surplus of 4.9% of GDP, versus 2.9% for Germany and 1.7% in the Eurozone as a whole. Even the external deficit, which in 2008 was the largest in the world, was substantially reduced in 2014 (−2.2% of GDP).[2]

Strange as it may sound, such adjustment progress was hardly a case for celebration. In fact, the two-party coalition that was charged with the implementation of the programme suffered a landslide defeat in the January 2015 elections. A new government of a Radical Left coalition and a Eurosceptic nationalist party was formed on the pledge to dismantle such policies.

On the debt front, Greece in 2012 enjoyed a sizeable reduction on the nominal value of outstanding sovereign bonds, but this was applied in a way that left most of the problems unresolved. The 'haircut', as the partial debt reduction came to be commonly known, had only had limited results, relieving the debt burden by a mere 14% of GDP and its effects were only temporary. As it currently stands at 177% of GDP, debt remains unsustainable all the way through. Ironically, it is almost 50 percentage points higher than its 2009 level at 129% of GDP, which triggered the original crisis and precipitated the austerity programme.

Even before the political shift to the Left, international markets had smelled the lack of robustness in the stabilization outcome and started beating their drum to the tune that new developments are on the way to tackle the mounting debt problem. Depending on each one's viewpoint of what should be done, Greece was considered to be left with two options: one to unilaterally default on her debt or else negotiate a new, larger 'haircut'. As this would mainly apply to the loans granted by Eurozone member states, it would require a new Memorandum and, inevitably, a new round of domestic political conflict and social unrest would unfold. With one in four unemployed and the other three being underpaid or not paid at all for long periods, any demand for further austerity would be a flame to a powder keg.

Impressively enough, the country's exit from the euro is advocated by the most conservative forces in the Eurozone and their most ardent opponents from the other end of the political spectrum in Greece. The former push for a Grexit because they cannot come to terms with the idea of a Europe that, in a time of crisis, offers support to those countries that found themselves deeper in its grip; the latter, because they do not want to coexist with a Europe that sets rules upon its members.

The Road to Grexit

Capitalizing on the distress and hardship brought about by the implementation of the Memorandum and the chronic shortcomings of the Greek economy, certain political forces, which have never been enthusiastic about Greece's European integration, started packaging the discontent caused by the economic crisis into a bid for restoring the drachma. However piecemeal or thinly documented their arguments may be, Grexit now appeals to a sizeable portion of Greece's society.

Faced with rampant unemployment and diminishing prospects, many households are blaming their plight on the euro and are eager to consider other options if they could give them a new chance. Trapped in unemployment, many young people realize that even if they found a job the pay would be minimal, and they would still have to pay for the older generations' debts and pensions for many decades. A new beginning would possibly erase a few burdens and open the road to them. Hard-pressed by recession and on the verge of ceasing operations, many businesses believe that a cheaper currency would help them re-enter the market. And, of course, those who borrowed from local banks might find it easier to repay loans in drachmas.

Grexit may not necessarily happen as a well-planned decision but might be driven by uncontrollable events and occur by accident; that makes it a 'Grexident'. The process would not be straightforward and there would be a period of several months, during which various other alternatives might be examined. Endless discussions with European authorities would be held in the hope that the possibility of reaching a last-minute consensus has not yet vanished, while internal reports of international organizations would warn for the impending chaos. It would be a game of ulterior motives, blame-allocation, political despair and hidden hopes. Greek and international media would pick up two leading players with opposing roles: a struggling Greece fighting for survival versus an unyielding Europe—and for that matter Germany—calling for a new round of fiscal adjustments and social sacrifices. Greece would not be alone in this drama: it will find explicit supporters in those political forces of Europe that have their own reasons for being at odds with the current situation in the Eurozone, as well as in other countries around the world that would be interested in seeing a new calamity for the euro and Europe in general. Hot on their heels would be a large number of international analysts who would propose unsolicited alternatives to the oncoming chaos, along with a bunch of investment houses that would like to see how far an internal split within the Eurozone could go and would be very interested to assess its financial consequences—for a fee and a return, as usual.

In this climate, the Greek government may nurture illusions that it can possibly borrow from other countries outside the Eurozone. In this hope, an aggressive stance towards the creditors might be viewed as fully backed and worth adopting. But when the time comes for the would-be supporters to actually grant the loans, they may demand high interest rates or put other odious terms, postponing pure solidarity for some other time. Sooner or later certain payments due by Greece will be missed and the possibility of a generalized default would loom ever larger. Fear would soon turn into panic, and, in a matter of days, the banks will be besieged by people anxious to withdraw their savings, as long as they were still denominated in euros.

Other payments may also not be honoured. At the moment that Greece refuses to repay its obligations to the three lending institutions, a credit event would be declared and then a unilateral default may be the next desperate move. Greece would be isolated in the European Union, and the next step would be that frustrated member states turn against Greece and demand that they are partially refunded by withholding structural funds and other EU handouts. At this point, the country would face a prolonged financial squeeze on top of the acute liquidity shortage.

Unchartered Waters

In practice, this option would be extremely painful. In an effort to deal with the banks' inability to reimburse deposits on a massive scale, the government would be forced to impose restrictions on capital withdrawals, thus infuriating depositors and exacerbating panic. In the following moments, more and more people will be demanding to withdraw their savings, albeit in vain, while all types of transactions would cease, as everyone would hoard money, preferring to create a 'nest-egg' in order to deal with the impending doom. The situation would spin out of control, and explode amidst social unrest. Leaving the common currency and massively issuing new inflationary notes would become the only available option. Being hostage to the events, the government would formally request the country's exit from the euro. Game over.

Afterwards, because everyone would claim reparations for the injustices suffered through adherence to the Memorandum's policies, the government of the day would be forced to print ample quantities of money in order to restore wages and pensions to their previous nominal levels, leading to successive devaluations, hyperinflation and a Latin American-style economic death-spiral. To avert this avalanche, someone might be tempted to put a ban on all demands, imposing an authoritarian regime.

Summing up, Greece's exit from the euro would neither help the European Union be more efficient nor make the Greeks more prosperous. It is more likely that a Grexit would, in the end, harm both sides: On the one hand, the European Union, because such a rift could easily be transmitted to other economies that may find themselves under pressure during some future crisis, thus keeping the Eurozone in a constant state of alert—a far cry from the region of stability it was meant to be. And on the other hand, the Greek citizens who, because the transition to a lower-value currency would trigger a prolonged process of falling incomes and persistent uncertainty, would suffer much more than they are today.

Setting the Argument Against

What is needed to face the current recession and social deprivation is not to change currency but to change policy, and how this might happen is examined in the rest of the book. To describe developments in Greece from the period preceding the crisis to nowadays, and address these issues, the book is structured as follows:

Chapter 1 explains that the threat of a Grexit has not been eliminated and may re-emerge in the event that a series of financial and social issues lead to an impasse. It traces the origins of the crisis to the inheritance of high debt levels from the 1980s and the inability of successive stabilization programmes to deal adequately with their dynamics.

Chapter 2 specifically discusses the failure of the policies that were implemented and that led to the current situation of deep recession, unemployment and ballooning debt.

Other Grexit arguments assume that, in economic terms, the euro was a wrong choice for the Greek economy from the very beginning, since it dragged it along a path it would not have otherwise taken. Chapter 3 challenges the contention that Greece should not have entered the Eurozone in the first place, and would have fared better had it kept its own currency. The analysis will prove the opposite: had Greece been left out of the Eurozone it would fare no better and, most likely, following the 2008 crisis it would be much worse off than it is today.

In Part II, chapter 4 assesses the theoretical and practical fallacies on which the adjustment programme was conceived, while Chapter 5 examines the role of recession in accelerating the debt burden. The dual risk of high unemployment and disinvestment is also discussed.

In Part III, chapter 6 describes the illusions invested in the Grexit scenario, in economic, social and geopolitical terms. Chapters 7 and 8 explore the crises in interwar Greece and today's Argentina, respectively, and demonstrate that no economic 'miracles' occurred simply because their currencies were rapidly devalued. In both cases, the economic recovery was limited and was, in any event only made possible when real wages were forced down, either by the imposition of authoritarian measures as in the case of Greece, or by soaring inflation, as in the case of Argentina.

In Part IV, chapter 9 suggests a different fiscal and investment policy mix, which could provide a faster way out of recession and secure debt sustainability without any risk of default. Chapters 10 and 11 delineate some critical reforms and institutional changes that could guarantee the viability of the stabilization effort and concurrently improve the sense of economic *egalité* among citizens and, more importantly, the younger generation. Chapter 12 describes the political economy of changing the currency and how the redistribution set about by the devaluation would lead to lower incomes and higher inequalities.

Finally, the Epilogue examines the new political reality that prevails in Greece with the government change after the January 2015 elections, and suggests a feasible strategy towards the European partners that can get the economy out of recession and rule out Grexit.

NOTES

1. Data are from Ameco database and IMF WEO Database.
2. European Commission, 2015. *European Economy, Vol. 2*. Economic Spring Forecast. Table 39, p. 173.

Part I

THE RUN-UP TO THE CRISIS

Chapter 1

Origins

How Greece Was Engulfed
in the Crisis

*The origins of the current malaise can be traced back to the overgrown pub-
lic debt in the 1980s. Though fiscal imbalances were partially corrected and
Greece joined the single currency in 2000, further reforms were delayed after
accession to the EMU and deficits gradually slipped beyond the limits of the
Stability and Growth Pact. The image of Greece in world markets was further tarnished by the fiscal audit that took place in 2005 and by the Goldman
Sachs swap executed in 2001 to reduce exposure to the Japanese yen. The
increasing incapacitation of the revenue-collection mechanism and a paral-
lel expansion of public spending prevented the government from effectively
responding to the 2008 global crisis, only to be followed by further expansionary policies by its successor.*

1.1. THE DEBT-ESCALATING PERIOD: 1980–1993

In 1981, Greece became a full-fledged member of the European Economic
Community (EEC) and this marked a whole new period for the economic and
political development of the country. Greece was one of the first non-found-
ing countries to start accession talks with the European Common Market as
early as 1961, but the process was abruptly suspended by the military dictatorship that lasted until 1974. Though membership of the EEC was rightly
viewed as an anchor for political and institutional stability for the newly
restored democracy, it nonetheless fed and multiplied uncertainties over the
ability of the Greek economy to survive in international markets.

It didn't take long for such fears to be substantiated. After a long period
of growth, Greece entered a period of recession in the late 1970s, not only
as a consequence of worldwide stagflation but also because—on its way to

11

integration with the common market—it had to dismantle its preferential system of subsidies, tariffs and state procurement by which several companies were kept profitable without being competitive. Soon after accession, many of them went bust and unemployment rose for the first time in many decades.

To accommodate some of the recessionary effects, fiscal policy turned expansionary. As a result, accession to the EEC strangely coincided with the unleashing of a demon that was thought to have been dormant thus far: *public debt*.

1.1.1. Accumulating Debt

In the early 1980s the government opted for a massive fiscal expansion that included demand-push policies to boost activity and the public underwriting of ailing private companies to maintain employment. The effect was quite predictable: private debt turned to a chronic hemorrhage of budget deficits without any supply-side improvements. Similarly, the expansion of demand simply led to more imports and higher prices. Activity got stuck and Greece ended up in a typical stagflation, perhaps the quickest assimilation to the European practices of the time.

Looking at Figure 1.1, there are three distinguishable phases for the dynamics of debt: The first covers the period 1980–1993 during which public debt rose from slightly above 20% of GDP towards 100% in 1993. The second phase spans the period 1994–2005 in which public debt ends up again at around 100% of GDP after two mild reductions in between. The third phase covers the period 2006–2011 during which public debt surpasses the 100% threshold, accelerates after 2008 and ends up at 129% of GDP in 2009, triggering the crisis.

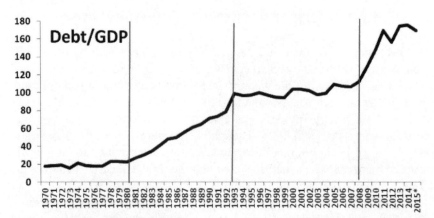

Figure 1.1   Greek Public Debt as Percent of GDP. *Source*: AMECO Eurostat. General government. Excessive deficit procedure, based on ESA 2010 and previous definitions. (Variable UDGG). For 2015, estimates.

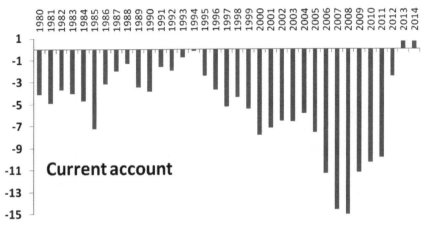

Figure 1.2   Current Account as Percent of GDP. *Source*: IMF WEO Database 2014.

The above periodicity broadly coincides with substantial shifts in the context of economic policies, as suggested by developments in the fiscal patterns and the current account shown in Figure 1.2. Fiscal developments are in more detail displayed in Figure 1.3 and briefly discussed below.

The main characteristic of the first phase was the substantial expansion of public spending and the concomitant rise in budget deficits and government debt. Revenues increased as a proportion of GDP, but were outpaced by the steadily growing expenditure. Both fiscal components appear to be volatile in election years (e.g. in 1981, 1985, 1989 and 1993), suggesting that a strong political cycle was put in motion with adverse consequences on stabilization efforts.

Since the collapse of Bretton Woods in 1972, the authorities had adopted the so-called system of a 'crawling peg' in which gradual nominal depreciation is used to offset inflation differentials with competitors and, thus, maintain a real exchange-rate target. After the government introduced an automatic wage indexation scheme in 1982, in order to immunize wages from the effects of inflation, a vicious circle was set off: the only effect of the exchange rate policy was to augment price, thus leading to wage increases that fuelled inflation and aggravated trade deficits all over again. To break the loop of depreciation and inflation, a discrete devaluation combined with a temporary wage freeze was implemented in 1983. Soon, however, the restrain effect was superseded by a new phase of expansion and pay rises as elections were approaching. Public debt simply climbed to higher levels.

The external deficit approached 8% of GDP in 1985: this was an alarming threshold as several Latin American economies with similar imbalances were serially collapsing at that time. A coherent stabilization programme

Figure 1.3   Primary Public Expenditure and Net Total Revenues as Percent of GDP.
Note: Revenues for 2014 not yet finalized. *Source*: Ministry of Finance, Greece. Budget Reports, various years.

was called for in October 1985 enforcing a discrete devaluation by 15%, a tough incomes policy and extensive cuts in public spending. The programme achieved a rise in revenues by cracking down on several tax-evasion practices and replacing previous indirect taxes with the more effective VAT system adopted by the EEC. Public debt was stabilized, but only until the programme was finally abandoned in 1988, after being fiercely opposed from within the government and the ruling party.

1.1.2. The First Fiscal Crisis

Two general elections in 1989 failed to secure a majority government, thus leading to the formation of coalition governments, an event that was hailed as a confirmation of political maturity and an opportunity to overcome partisan differences on major issues. But these self-indulgent expectations were short-lived, as stabilization policies are notoriously difficult to be implemented through party coalitions because each party tries to avoid the cost falling on its own constituency. Greece was no exception to this rule, and the economy suffered a major setback in 1989–1990 that was far more serious than previous fiscal failures.

Two episodes are characteristic of how rhetoric designed to please everybody in combination with naïve policies can lead to disaster: despite looming deficits in 1989, the coalition government decided to abolish prison terms for major tax arrears, hoping to induce offenders to reconsider their strategy.

As might be expected, the move had the opposite effect and was rather taken as a signal of relaxed monitoring in the future, thus encouraging further evasion.

Another bizarre policy was to cut import duties for car purchases by impoverished repatriates returning to Greece after the collapse of the Soviet Union. The measure was viewed as a gesture to facilitate mobility back in the motherland, but it was quickly turned into a black-market scam. For a small bribe, immigrants would purchase luxury cars only to resell them immediately to rich clients, who thus avoided paying any duties for importing them into the country.

With revenues collapsing, the country began to suffer a major strain in public finances until a majority government was elected in 1990 and enacted a new stabilization programme. Despite substantial cuts in spending and a rise in revenues, public debt as a ratio to GDP continued to rise, this time due to the higher cost of borrowing worldwide and a stagnant output. The sharp rise in 1993, in particular, was due to the inclusion of extensive debts initially contracted by public companies under state guarantees but finally underwritten by the Treasury. The subsequent fiscal consolidation significantly improved the current account and the rarity of a balanced external position was briefly achieved in 1994.

In the 1980s, extensive wage increases took place both in the public sector, where the government capitulated to aggressive trade union demands, and in the private sector by raising minimum wage levels and establishing collective bargaining agreements. As shown in Figure 1.4, the wage share reached nearly 60% of GDP in the early 1980s but then declined as a result

Figure 1.4 The Wage Share in Total Economy. *Source*: Ameco Eurostat.

of the stabilization programme in 1985–1987. After a blip in the period of fiscal instability in 1989, it kept on falling to around 50% in the early 1990s.

1.2. DEBT STABILIZATION AND EMU MEMBERSHIP

Although Greece was a signatory of the Maastricht Treaty in 1991, it was far from obvious whether, how and when the country would comply with the nominal convergence criteria required to join the Economic and Monetary Union. Public deficits and inflation were galloping at two-digit levels and there was great uncertainty about the viability of the exchange rate system.[1] In May 1994, capital controls were lifted in compliance with European guide-lines and this prompted a fierce speculation in the forex market. Interest rates reached particularly high levels and the Central Bank of Greece exhausted most of its reserves to stave off the attack. This episode proved to be a turning point for the country's determination to pursue accession to EMU in order to be shielded by the common currency and to avoid similar attacks in the future. Soon afterwards the 'Convergence Programme' was adopted with a specific timeframe to satisfy the Maastricht criteria. A battery of reforms in the banking and the public sectors was also included.

Nevertheless, international markets were not impressed and remained unconvinced about exchange rate viability. At the eruption of the Asian crisis in 1997, spreads rose dramatically and—after months of credit shortages—Greece finally decided to devalue the drachma by 12.5% in March 1998 and subsequently enter the Exchange Rate Mechanism wherein it had to stay for two years. Greece obviously was not yet ready to join the first round of Euro-zone countries in 1998, thus a transition period was granted allowing her to comply with the convergence criteria by the end of 1999.

After depreciation, credibility was further enhanced by structural reforms and reduced state borrowing so that when the Russian crisis erupted in August 1998, the currency came under very little pressure. Public expendi-ture was kept below the peaks it had reached in the previous decade and was increasingly outpaced by rising revenues and various one-off receipts. Tax collection was enhanced by the introduction of a framework setting a mini-mum turnover on SMEs, the elimination of a vast number of tax allowances, the imposition of a new levy on large real-estate property and a thorough reorganization of the auditing system. Proceeds were further augmented by public company privatizations and, as a result, public debt fell to 93% of GDP in 1999. Although still higher than the 60% threshold required by the Euro-pean Treaty, Greece benefited from the convenient interpretation that debt suffices '*to lean toward that level*', previously used by other highly indebted countries—such as Italy and Belgium—on their own way to enter the EMU.

1.2.1. The Implementation of Market Reforms

In the 1980s, structural reforms were hardly on the agenda of Greek economic policy. In fact, for most of the period the term was a misnomer and used to describe further state intervention in economic activity, rather than market-oriented policies as practised by other European countries. Market reforms were introduced for the first time in 1986 and were aimed at the modernization of the outmoded banking and financial system, in compliance with European directives. A major reform in social security took place for the first time in 1992, curbing early retirement and excessively generous terms on the pension/income ratios.

Throughout the 1990s, various reform programmes were aimed at restructuring public companies whose chronic deficits had contributed to earlier fiscal crises. Privatizations were attempted through direct sales of state-owned utilities as the quick way to reduce debt and cut deficits. Despite some initial success, the programme was fiercely opposed by the trade unions of public companies and eventually led to the demise of the government. Privatizations were conveniently brandished as illegal sell-outs, and it took a few more years for the topic to gain political legitimacy and reappear on the reform agenda.

A new wave of reforms was launched after 1996 in the course of the Convergence Programme. State banks were privatized or merged, dozens of outmoded organizations were closed down, and—taking advantage of the stock market bonanza—a series of IPOs provided capital and restructuring finance to several public utilities. As company road-shows had to be organized in international markets, a new generation of management teams were appointed to replace party apparatchiks and implement further restructuring and modernization. Other structural changes included the lifting of closed-shop practices in shipping, the entry of more players into the ascending mobile telephony market and a series of efforts to make the economic environment more conducive to entrepreneurship and job creation.

1.2.2. Debt Persistence

Despite having achieved substantial primary surpluses throughout 1994–2002—and in 1999 in particular—public debt fell only slightly over the same period. The main reason was that primary surpluses were not sufficiently large and systematic, nor were privatizations extensive enough to cause a major one-off reduction of public obligations. Another reason was that, during the same period, the government had to issue bonds to accumulate a sufficient stock of assets for the Bank of Greece as a prerequisite for its inclusion in the Eurosystem, and this capital injection led to a substantial increase in public debt without affecting the deficit.

Public debt suffered further rises by foreign currency volatility that was augmenting its domestic value, the underwriting of indebted public utilities that were at the end unable to repay their loans, or the rapid expansion of military spending. Lacking a systematic policy of primary surpluses sufficient enough to dispose of public debt, stabilization was frequently relying on *ad hoc* practices to control its rise. Some of these practices invited a lot of criticism—both from domestic opposition and international organizations—and deeply tarnished the credibility of public finances. Two of the most publicized cases are considered below.

1.3. STABILIZATION TARNISHED

1.3.1. The Fiscal Audit

In January 1996, a new government was sworn in to replace the ailing prime minister.[2] The newly nominated PM was an outspoken critic of defence expenditure and planned to cut it so as to lower the fiscal burden and, thus, accelerate the process of joining the EMU. But during the process of the government getting parliamentary approval, a military stand-off with Turkey over an islet in the Aegean broke out, causing the death of three Greek pilots and risking further escalation of hostilities. The incident was finally brought under control, but the bitterness that prevailed afterwards in the public opinion made the defence cuts untenable. The new PM withdrew such a pledge from his programmatic statement and Greece entered a period of increased military spending.

Defence procurement subsequently rose to well above 4% of GDP per year, substantially stretching public finances at a time when even more consolidation was needed. In line with Eurostat rules, the burden was recorded in the debt account at the time of ordering but only gradually in the current expenditure along the time pattern of actually delivering the equipment.

This practice created a considerable lag in the debt–deficit adjustment and, the government that was elected in 2004 enforced a massive revision of the deficit figures by retroactively augmenting public spending on the date of ordering. The motivation behind this exercise was twofold: first to defame its political opponent, which had been the party in charge at the time of Greece's entry to EMU; second to create a threatening picture of public finances so as to avoid delivering on its massive pre-electoral promises on wage increases, lower taxes and even more public sector jobs.

This prompted a major dispute over the quality and integrity of the statistics of public finances in Greece. Though a decision by Eurostat in 2006 made the delivery-based rule obligatory for all countries, Greece did not withdraw the self-inflicted revision.[3] As a consequence, and in an awkward demonstration of political interference, deficit data were statistically augmented for 2000–2004 and then scaled-back for 2005–2006 relative to what they should have been otherwise.

1.3.2. The Goldman Sachs Swap[4]

A less well-known reason why the public debt was prevented from falling as a ratio to GDP was the strong appreciation of the Japanese Yen in the beginning of the 2000s. After the speculative crisis in its forex market in 1994, Greece faced a prohibitive cost of borrowing in international markets and turned to loans in Japanese currency that were available at very low rates. But this facility turned sour when the Japanese currency appreciated at a time that Greece had to classify its debt in euro terms after entering EMU in 2000. In June 2001, the rate had reached a low of around 100 yen/€, an appreciation of 30% compared to around 130 yen/€ that had prevailed in early 1999 when the euro was launched. By swapping an amount of yen-denominated loans with euro-denominated bonds at retroactive rates, such a sizeable difference was offering an opportunity to reduce its current value by alleviating the exogenous deterioration of the debt burden.

Therefore, Greece—like several other Eurozone countries—entered a currency swap in June 2001 on a notional amount of around €10 billion, thus generating a nominal 'relief' of €2.8 billion, roughly proportional to the above-mentioned appreciation of the yen. This amount was equivalent to 1.7% of GDP and would be balanced *quid pro quo* with a gradual burdening over time through increased interest payments of around 0.15% of GDP per year determined within a given band of Euribor rates. The overall fiscal position remained unchanged in present value terms and the swap would be fully reversed at maturity at 2019. At that point, total repayments would amount to around €5.9 billion at current value, which is 2.10 times the relief, slightly over the ratio implied in a transaction of normal bonds with the same 20-year maturity.

However, two things went wrong rendering the above assumptions invalid. The first was that, following the terrorist attacks in the United States on September 11, 2001, the Eurosystem conducted several fine-tuning operations in order to smooth developments in the euro money market and raise liquidity. This drove Euribor below the low band, thus making interest payments at the predetermined levels costlier than they would have been if rates were driven by the open market.[5] The swap was restructured twice in response to these changes, but then another drawback loomed: the yen started to *depreciate* fast and by the end of 2002 it had fallen below the historical rate on which the swap was contracted. To put it simply, the exchange rate burden of yen-denominated debt would have been automatically diminished in euro terms even if it had remained un-swapped. The scheme was restructured again and finally exchanged by the National Bank of Greece in early 2009 at an amount of €5.1 billion, corresponding to the adjusted cumulative repayments.

The first swap was in no violation whatsoever of Eurostat practices at the time, but later rules became far more stringent. Thus, when the 2009 swap transaction was submitted as collateral to obtain liquidity from the Eurosystem, it was met with suspicion and heavy criticism from the ECB. The situation became more embarrassing as the government invited Goldman Sachs in late 2009 for advice on emergency financing, while at the same time appointed as head of the Debt Management Office a previous employee of the bank, who also appeared to be in charge of the swap transaction with the National Bank.[6] Despite all the clarifications provided during parliamentary questions, the story fed all kinds of imagination in the witch-hunting atmosphere that prevailed in the post-2008 period, and Greece was engulfed in yet another round of statistical malpractice. The Greek economy was pictured as unable not only to face its problems but even to record them properly, making it the perfect prey for political and market speculation.

Although the transaction had no bearing on the statistics for 1999 on which EMU entry was assessed, Greece suffered extensively from criticisms that mistook the swap as a ploy to circumvent a proper evaluation prior to the adoption of the common currency. Even today, politically motivated opinions disregard the facts and deliberately claim that the swap was essential in securing Greece's entry into the EMU.[7] Summing up, the transaction proved to be a costly complexity that conferred few and temporary gains in managing the Greek debt, and great—though mostly unfounded—disrepute for its accounts. The swap effect on the debt was very small and did not alter its evolution in any fundamental account. Values shown in Figure 1.1 are net of swap effects, and this explains the peak in 2001.

1.4. POST-EMU FATIGUE

1.4.1. Reform Slowdown

After 2000, several public utilities and real-estate properties were privatized, and even the strong state monopoly on the electricity market was relaxed. Proceeds from privatizations peaked in 1999, but subsequently fell as a result of the contraction in capital markets after the *dotcom* bubble and the global recession in 2003.[8] In other areas, the reform process slowed down due to direct political opposition and, in this regard, Greece emulated several other Eurozone members in exhibiting a *'post-EMU fatigue'*.

A major setback was the attempt in 2001 to implement a major reform of the pension system. Fierce reaction from trade unions and key members of the ruling socialist party led to serious social confrontations and the reform was finally abandoned. Although replaced by a watered-down version a year later, the backlash marred the government's willingness to subsequently intervene in the social security system. Two mild reforms followed in 2006 and 2010, but none was adequate enough to make the system get rid of inequalities, major inefficiencies and widening deficits that continued to exert a substantial pressure on public finances. A major Tax Reform was enacted in 2003 to simplify archaic procedures, curtail offshore tax havens and speed up settlements of arrears, but was suspended a few months later by the new government coming to office after the March 2009 elections.

Fatigue spread more widely after the Olympic Games in 2004. With the exception of the sale of Greek Telecom to the Deutsche telecom company and the privatization of the national air carrier after a decade of failed attempts, most other reforms consisted of limited-scale IPOs with no structural spillovers to the rest of the economy. When the 2008 crisis erupted, the reform agenda was in limbo.

1.4.2. The Current Account Deficit

After the Eurozone became operational, hardly any attention was paid to current account imbalances, regarding any deficit country or Greece in particular. Even after national external deficits had reached huge proportions, the problem of external disparities in the Eurozone continued to remain surprisingly unnoticed from a policy viewpoint. It was only in the aftermath of the 2008 crisis that—with *ex post* wisdom—policy bodies in the European Union started emphasizing the adverse effects that external imbalances may have on the sustainability of the common currency.[9]

The reason for this complacency was not merely that devaluations were ruled out by the common currency. A widespread—and unwisely convenient—view held that external imbalances were mostly demand-driven effects and, as such, they would sooner or later dissipate as a result of ongoing fiscal adjustment in member states. Chief IMF economist, Oliver Blanchard, was asked in 2002 whether 'countries such as Portugal or Greece should worry about and take measures to reduce their Current Account deficits.' Astonishingly, as it sounds today, he did 'conclude, to a first order, that *they should not'* (emphasis added). A few years later, current account deficits were steadily increasing and—overturning his previous optimism—the same economist urged for immediate action otherwise '. . . implications can be bad'.[10] And indeed they were.

Although it improved for a while after the country joined the EMU, the subsequent vast deterioration of the Greek current account played a crucial role in inviting the global economic crisis home. The reason behind the initial containment was that factor income flows from abroad increased as a result of extensive Greek foreign direct investment in neighbouring countries, while labour immigration kept domestic wage increases initially at bay. The deficit started to deteriorate after 2004 for a combination of reasons: domestic demand peaked in the post-Olympics euphoria; inflation differentials with other Eurozone countries widened, thus cutting competitiveness vis-à-vis other member states; and, on top, the euro appreciated further, cutting competitiveness with the rest of the world.

1.4.3. Competitiveness Eroded

Unit labour costs increased and, as shown in Figure 1.5, the relevant index rose by 10% in the period 1999–2010. In the same diagram, it is worth noting that a similar erosion of competitiveness took place in *all* other Eurozone countries that subsequently entered bailout agreements (Ireland by 12% and Portugal by 8%) or were considered to be at the risk of seeking one (Spain by 9% and Italy by 8%).

Greek unit labour costs increased by 27% vis-à-vis Germany, causing significant bilateral imbalances. However, this erosion was gradual and cannot be regarded as the single reason for the rapid deterioration experienced after 2006. Other factors affecting the investment environment, such as the quality

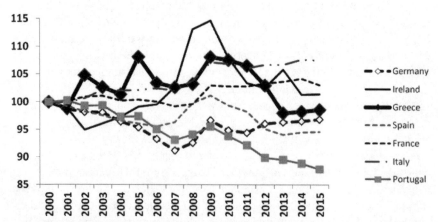

Figure 1.5   Competitiveness Indicators Based on Unit Labour Cost. (Ratio of compensation per employee to nominal GDP per person employed.) *Source*: Ameco Eurostat. Real unit labour costs: total economy (QLCD). Index rebased at year 2000, value =100.

of the regulatory framework, the elimination of corruption practices and the overall effectiveness of the government might as well have been crucial in shaping productivity and competitiveness. And here laid yet one more post-EMU shortcoming.

Right after her accession to the EMU, Greece improved its competitiveness ranking worldwide. From being one of the last-ranking countries during the previous decades, it gradually rose to more respectable positions. According to the Global Competitiveness Index compiled by the World Economic Forum, Greece in 2003 was ranked 35th thanks to improved infrastructures and institutions, macroeconomic stability and the dissipation of political strife and protestation. But this was not to last for long. As displayed in Figure 1.6, the country started to be downgraded again in the post-Olympic period, losing as many positions as it had managed to gain on its way towards the common currency.

These developments were pivotal to Greece's poor performance in attracting foreign direct investment in spite of the substantial fall in interest rates and the facilitation of capital flows within the Eurozone. FDI expressed as percent of GDP hardly improved during the last decade relative to the 1980s. Its composition has also changed, as most of FDI inflows were directed to non-manufacturing sectors. An increasing allocation to the real-estate sector boosted domestic demand and further aggravated the strain on the current account.

It is a well-established fact that when new investments are directed mainly to the tradable sectors, this leads to substantial productivity improvements and net exports gains. In contrast, investments going mostly into the real-estate sector boost aggregate demand, raise prices, cause the real exchange rate to appreciate and hinder competitiveness. These developments manifest

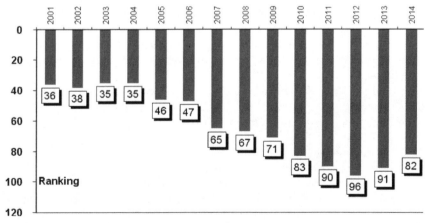

Figure 1.6 The Global Competitiveness Index. *Source*: reports.weforum.org/global-competitiveness-report-2014-2015/rankings.

a major failure of Greece—and for that matter of other crisis-hit Eurozone countries—to exploit the post-EMU expansion in capital flows in order to upgrade technology and expand production.[11]

***

The preceding analysis suggests that the Greek economy, even after joining the common currency, was still characterized by inherent deficiencies, most of which stemmed from the inability to control public finances systematically and to develop strong comparative advantages. The high debt level created by the populist policies of the 1980s continued to loom large over the economy, despite some improvements that took place around the time of EMU membership. In the absence of adequate adjustment to the pressure of globalization, the economy remained vulnerable to external shocks and, when they erupted after 2007, it was ill-prepared to deal with them.

NOTES

1. For a detailed analysis of this period, see Christodoulakis (1994).

2. Prime Minister Andreas Papandreou resigned in January 1996 and was replaced by Costas Simitis after a decision taken by the parliamentary party group. Simitis was elected as president of the party in the June 1996 congress.

3. Mamatzakis (2014) acknowledges the rules on the statistical procedures but nevertheless fails to account for their impact on correcting the deficit figures.

4. The swap was conducted in July 2001 and a clarification is due here. The author of this book served as Minister of Finance between late October 2001 and early March 2004. Thus he was neither involved whatsoever in the making of the first swap, nor in its later transformation and sale to the National Bank of Greece.

5. As reported by the ECB Monthly Bulletin (2001, September, p. 7).

6. For more details, see the article by C. Mollenkamp in the *Wall Street Journal*, 25 Feb. 2010. http://www.wsj.com/articles/SB10001424052748703791504575075079903903971986

7. A recent demonstration of such distortion of facts is an article by Tsamadias (2014).

8. For an analysis of reforms in Greece over the period 1990–2008, see Christodoulakis (2012).

9. See for example EC (2009).

10. Blanchard and Giavazzi (2002), and Blanchard (2006), respectively.

11. For further details, see a study by Christodoulakis and Sarantides (2015) who use the differentiation in composition and the asymmetry in the volumes of FDI to explain the diverging patterns of external balances in the Eurozone countries.

Chapter 2

Complacency

Was the 2010 Bailout **Really** *Inevitable?*

In 2008, Greece started to come under increasing credit pressure: spreads were widening, while rating agencies had started to issue warnings and downgrade the country. Yet, the expectation was that a pre-emptive fiscal consolidation could still correct the situation before running out of control. But the early elections in October 2009 had two adverse consequences: the outgoing government refrained from taking some early consolidation measures; while the incoming one was promising that a further expansion was feasible. This chapter describes the new government's failure to organize a consolidation programme and how it was quickly overwhelmed by liquidity shortages that necessitated the bailout agreement.

2.1. UNPREPARED FOR THE 2008 CRISIS

The fiscal decline started with the disappearance of primary surpluses after 2003 and culminated with skyrocketing public expenditure and the collapse of revenues in 2009, as has been shown in Figure 1.3. Revenues declined in 2005 as a result of a major cut in the corporate tax rate from 35% to 25% and extensive inattention to the collection of revenues.

Such decisions made it increasingly evident that stabilizing the economy was not a policy priority for the government, and further actions soon confirmed this assumption: concerned over the rising deficits in 2007, the government sought a fresh mandate to redress public finances but—despite securing a clear victory—no such action was taken after the election. Just a few months before the global crisis actually erupted, the government claimed that the Greek economy was '*sufficiently fortressed*' and would stay immune to the reverberations of any external shocks. Even after September 2008, the government was for a long time ambivalent as to whether it should implement a harsh programme to stem further fiscal deterioration or expand public spending to fight off the prospect of recession. A final compromise, at the end of the year, included a consumption stimulus combined with a bank rescue plan of €5 billion and a pledge to raise extra revenues. The first two were quickly implemented, while the latter was forgotten.

Weakened by internal divisions, the government continued to be indecisive about what exactly to do and, after a defeat in the European elections in May 2009, opted for yet another general election in October 2009 asking for a fresh mandate to address the mounting economic problems. In practice, the election period provided an opportunity for a further spending spree rather than for preparing methods for containing it. The fiscal consequences were stunning: total public expenditure was pumped up by nearly five percentage units of GDP by the end of 2009, as depicted in Figure 1.3. The rise was entirely due to consumption as public investment remained the same as the year before, at 4.1% of GDP.[1] In absolute terms, the spree looked even more excessive as public consumption increased twofold in comparison to the amount of €31 billion back in 2003.

Total receipts in 2009 collapsed by another 4% of GDP as a result of widespread neglect in regard to collection and auditing. The general government deficit spiralled and its figure was serially revised from an estimated 6.7% of GDP before the elections in June to 12.4% in October 2009, finally jumping to 15.4% of GDP by the end of the year. It was only then that European authorities stopped standing by and issued a number of warnings. But the tide was too strong to be thwarted by paperwork and tough talking.

2.2. THE THREAT OF EXTERNAL DEFICITS

The 2008 global financial crisis revealed that countries with sizeable current account deficits are vulnerable to international market pressures because they risk having a 'sudden stoppage' of liquidity. Recent studies show that highly indebted EMU countries with large external deficits experienced the highest sovereign bond yield spreads. Along this line, Nobel Prize winner Paul Krugman suggested that the crisis in the southern Eurozone countries had rather little to do with fiscal imbalances and rather more to do with the sudden shortage of capital inflows required to finance their huge external deficits.[2]

This explains why, immediately after the crisis, sovereign spreads peaked mainly in economies with large external imbalances, such as Ireland, Spain, Portugal and the Baltic countries, which were under little or no pressure from fiscal deficits.[3] In contrast, countries with substantially higher debt burdens but without external imbalances, such as Belgium and Italy, experienced only a small increase in their borrowing costs at that time.

Greece happened to have a dismal record on both deficits, and its exposure to the international credit stoppage was soon transformed into a debt crisis. The current account went in free-fall after 2006 when three factors intensified: domestic credit expansion accelerated and disposable incomes were enhanced by the tax cuts, while capital inflows from the Greek shipping sector peaked as a result of the global glut and the huge rise in Chinese freight. The external deficit exceeded 14% of GDP in 2007 and 2008—still no warning was voiced by any authority, domestic or European. In fact quite the opposite happened: responding to pleas of car dealers, the Greek government decided to reduce surcharges on imported vehicles in an attempt to revive demand failing to notice the pro-cyclical character of the measure. Replicating the events of 1989, the unfortunate attempt to facilitate car purchases in order to favour particular groups caused again a significant deterioration of both the external and the public deficit. In addition, nobody could have missed the signals this gave out about the true priorities of the government, leading to the aforementioned pre-electoral spending spree.

2.3. POST-ELECTION INACTION

In spite of the gathering storm in the autumn of 2009, the newly elected government was far from determined to push for an immediate fiscal consolidation, completely ignoring the warning signs worldwide. One constraint was set by its own pre-electoral rhetoric that *'Lefta yparhoun'*, meaning that there is money out there, and can be discovered and finance expansionary policies. Another was its ideological inclination to uncritically endorse trade union demands in public enterprises, instead of implementing restructuring business plans and privatizations. Before the elections, the party leadership had pledged to re-nationalize the Greek Telecom that was partly sold to the Deutsche telecom, and also annul the sale of transportation facilities in the Port of Piraeus to Chinese interests. Though the government finally backed off from its pre-electoral pledges, it succumbed to a lavish compensation to the employees in exchange for agreeing to the privatization.

Seeing that no appropriate action had been taken to deal with the situation, all of the three major rating agencies serially downgraded the Greek economy in December 2009: Fitch from A- to BBB+, Standard & Poor's from A-plus to BBB-plus, and Moody's from A1 to A2 category.[4] It was the first time in ten years that the country had seen its rating pushed below an A grade. As cited in the Fitch report, the downgrading was due to 'the weak credibility of fiscal institutions and the policy framework . . . exacerbated by uncertainty over the prospects for a balanced and sustained economic recovery'.[5] This development triggered massive credit default swaps in international markets and the crisis started looming more threateningly. Still, a few days later, the government surprised everybody by announcing that the Budget Plan for 2010 endorsed an *expansion* of public expenditure and completely *excluded* further privatizations, rather than the other way around. It was an incredible demonstration of parting with reality.

The problem Greece faced at that time was an acute shortage of credit financing for its deficit, but not yet a question of debt sustainability as later turned out to be the case. In this regard, a significant opportunity to diffuse the crisis was missed by the government and the European authorities alike and this is explained below. In order to reduce the risk of spillover effects to other markets after the 2008 credit crunch, the ECB had invited private banks of Euro member states to obtain low-cost liquidity by using sovereign bonds from their asset portfolios as collateral securitization.[6] As a result of this credit facilitation, yields on Treasury bills remained exceptionally low. But instead of being shielded from world markets by borrowing cheaply in the short term and thus gaining time to redress the fiscal situation, the government kept on issuing long maturities despite the escalation of costs. This had dramatic consequences on how international markets assessed the criticality of the situation and its handling. Commenting on the cost of confusion in Greece, Martin Feldstein aptly noted:

> What started as a concern about a Greek *liquidity problem*—in other words, about the ability of Greece to have the cash to meet its next interest payments— became *a solvency problem*, a fear that Greece would never be able to repay its existing and accumulating debt (emphases added).[7]

The two other countries, Ireland and Portugal, that had also sought a bail-out, exited the supervision regime in 2013 and 2014, respectively. Both have experienced a much milder recession: Portugal's GDP contracted by around 4% relative to the pre-crisis level, while Ireland has already achieved an even higher level of growth. When Ireland exited the bailout programme at the end of 2013, public debt was running at 123% of GDP. Six months later, Portugal followed suit and exited the programme with public debt running at 129% of GDP. At such levels, their public debts were both considered as affordably sustainable. The irony is that the crisis in Greece was triggered when the public debt was around the same proportion to GDP, but at that time it was viewed as threateningly unsustainable. The explanation is probably that Greece, as other countries, was facing a liquidity crisis rather than a solvency question as pointed out by the analysis in chapter 3.

One mistake led to another: A further aggravating factor was the European authorities' unpreparedness and unwillingness to react promptly[8] to the rapid isolation of Greece from international bond markets. A clear manifestation of misjudging the situation took place when the European Central Bank refused to grant collateral status[9] for all denominations of Greek sovereign bonds supplied by commercial banks in exchange for liquidity. As this came days after Greece was downgraded by the rating agencies in December 2009, it sparked new fears that a default was imminent. In early 2010, as borrowing costs started to escalate across both short- and long-term maturities, Greece had become a front-page story worldwide and the countdown began. The initial aloofness shown by EU authorities towards the emergency approaching a Eurozone country was dissipated only when it became clear that the difficulties in servicing the Greek debt might quickly propagate into the banking system of other European states and cause another painful recession in their economies, just when they were about to exit the previous slump. Thus in March 2010 the ECB conceded that Greek sovereign bonds would finally enjoy full collateral treatment for another three years regardless of rating status. But by then it was too late for the prevailing view of Greece at the brink of insolvency to be reversed.

Despite the ECB's belated generosity, the government was financially exhausted and in April 2010 sought a bailout. After sweeping negotiations, a joint EU and IMF loan of €110 billion was finally agreed in May 2010 to be granted to Greece as a substitute for unreachable market borrowing. The condition was that Greece implement a Memorandum of ambitious deficit targets and structural reforms, aimed at ensuring fiscal credibility and restore competitiveness and growth.

***

This analysis shows that Greece could have probably mitigated—if not mostly avoided—the intensity of the austerity programme if some early consolidation had been agreed on to stabilize deficits and calm the markets worldwide. The lack of defensive measures, as well as the government's inexperience in how to handle the impending crisis, was hidden behind a convenient simplification that the problem was impossible to fix anyway. This sparked a debate—both in Greece and abroad—about all the delays and inefficiencies that had led to the bailout agreement and how they stemmed from the fact that Greece was tightly constrained by the common currency with no room for manoeuvre. Had the country not entered the Eurozone—the pretentious argument goes on—adjustment could have been fast and efficient. Thus, the question of whether Greece should have joined the euro in the first place is discussed in the next chapter.

NOTES

1. Details on how public spending ballooned are given in Christodoulakis (2010).
2. Krugman (2011).
3. For a discussion of the effects of the credit crunch in emerging markets with large current account deficits see Shelburne (2008).
4. The ratings can be found in http://en.wikipedia.org/wiki/Greek_debt_crisis_ timeline.
5. According to the Financial Times, December 8, 2009. http://www.ft.com/intl/ cms/s/0/2763a1d6-e3fc-11de-b2a9-00144feab49a.html#axzz3YcILw5Rh.
6. For an assessment of this policy, see De Grauwe (2010).
7. Feldstein (2012).
8. This is in contrast with the readiness shown in the cases of Hungary, Latvia and Romania that were quickly assisted by IMF and European Union funds in 2008 and 2009.
9. After the 2008 credit crunch, the ECB invited the member states' private banks to obtain low-cost liquidity using sovereign bonds rated A+ or above as collateral securitization. De Grauwe (2010), commenting on the extension of bonds collateralization, argued that the decision of ECB was '. . . a major contribution . . . to reducing the risk of spill over to other markets'.

Chapter 3

Reinventing the Past

Should Greece Have Joined the Euro?

Many, both in Greece and abroad, argue that the country shouldn't have joined the Economic and Monetary Union in the first place. To show how little different a course outside EMU would have been in terms of policy flexibility, this chapter provides a simple comparison: the main macroeconomic indicators of Greece are juxtaposed against six countries of the European Union which have not yet joined the common currency. In each period, Greece's actual outcome is compared with the best and worst performance of the non-Eurozone group and is found to fall within the mini max band. Other issues regarding the entry exchange rate and the timing of accession are also discussed.

3.1. THE ARGUMENTS AGAINST AND A RESPONSE

The persisting failure of the austerity programme to contain the explosive rise of debt and unemployment fuelled arguments in support of exiting the euro. This is due to the perception that many people rush to equate the imposition and outcome of the programme as a consequence of the adoption of the single currency. In reality, the programme and the currency are two different systems and the application of one does neither require nor inescapably lead to the existence of the other. Adjustment programmes have often been implemented in countries with their own national currency when external deficits have grown explosively or their monetary policy has become untrustworthy. In many cases, these programmes have included prescriptions similar to those implemented in Greece, and quite often they led to similar failures. So, it is important to explore the specific causes of the severe recession of the Greek economy, in order to demonstrate that they themselves are the result of erroneous policy choices and not of the single currency's adoption as will be discussed in more detail in Part II.

Before doing this, however, it is critical to respond to the arguments that Greece shouldn't have joined the euro in the first place. Although these beliefs are rarely formulated in a cohesive manner, their common premise is that most of the problems facing the country after 2000 were generated, or grew out of proportion, as a result of drachma's entry in the Economic and Monetary Union. Strangely, such views never elaborate whether non-participation would enable Greece to implement a more intensive fiscal adjustment or simply allow her to ignore the need for consolidation and expand further. In the latter case, the crisis would have come earlier and more frequently; in the former they should also support—rather than oppose—the Memorandum as offering an opportunity for completing the job. In fact, Greece—had it not joined the euro—not only would not have avoided the adjustments it eventually had to make, but their cost would be even higher. As the comparison below is going to show, its problems would, most probably, be more intense; not more moderate. In the following, the most frequent arguments as to why Greece's euro entry was a mistake are enumerated, along with a brief response to each one.

3.1.1. The exchange rate, at which Greece joined the single currency (i.e. 340.5 drachmas per euro), was overvalued and, thus, condemned the country to a continuing loss of international competitiveness

The entry exchange rate resulted from the 12% pre-emptive devaluation in March 1998. After that, the value of the drachma had to fluctuate within a narrow band, without any further steep adjustment being allowed. In fact, there were no downward pressures in the spot exchange market until the country's EMU accession, suggesting that this exchange rate was fair and acceptable to traders. Had the exchange rate been more extensively depreciated, foreign debt would immediately be augmented and the purchasing power of salaries and pensions would have fallen by almost the same percentage. Given that inflation would also soar, nominal interest rates would soon have to follow suit. As a result, the relevant criterion of the interest rate not surpassing a certain level would be violated. Greece would never qualify for EMU entry.

3.1.2. Before Greece joined the euro, the drachma had a strong purchasing power and households were satisfied. Post-euro though, the extortionate rounding of consumer staple prices led to high inflation, which eroded the households' purchasing power

Admittedly, Greek households became better off after 1995, but this was simply because the drachma had been stabilized in the run-up to joining the euro.

In other words, the purchasing constancy of the drachma was not a feature of its 'national currency' status but, on the contrary, was precisely due to the fact of already being on a path of losing its independence. It is edifying to recall events of the late 1970s and 1980s, when the drachma was truly an independent national currency but the purchasing power of salaries and pensions was evaporating month by month due to rampant inflation.

However, the introduction of the euro did, indeed, disrupt the households' daily consumption patterns, both in Greece and in other countries. Despite the double display of prices and continuous market inspections, extensive profiteering in low-price items tarnished the entire process and made households distrustful of the new currency. Even so, there were also substantial reductions in the price of durable goods, which partly offset the losses caused by all this profiteering. Notwithstanding any transition-induced problems, the gains generated by stability and the lower cost of money eventually benefitted the majority of households, although in certain cases also led to easy borrowing with disastrous consequences.

3.1.3. As a result of joining the euro, Greece had to undergo a fiscal adjustment, that took resources away from vital social needs and development programmes

In the 1990s, Greece's economy featured large deficits, double-digit inflation and a rapidly growing debt. Regardless of joining the euro or not, the country had to carry out a major fiscal adjustment. Attempting to do so outside the Eurozone would have been a much more precarious and painful exercise, since lending rates would have remained at higher levels. On the contrary, the prospect of joining the single currency led to a substantial reduction of borrowing costs, and the adjustment process was accelerated. Instead of being deprived of resources for growth, the country actually managed to claim and secure increased funding from the European Union structural funds in order to finance infrastructure, training programmes and investment projects, all of them thanks to the development process of successfully joining the euro.

3.1.4. Overall, the abolition of the national currency deprived Greece of the option to adjust the exchange rate in order to restore competitiveness and avoid the deterioration of the external deficit

Perhaps surprisingly, following Greece's adoption of the euro, the current account actually improved instead of deteriorating. The external deficit fell from 7.80% of GDP in 2000 to 5.70% in 2003, an improvement of more than two percentage points.[1] In fact, had this pace of improvement been sustained in the following years, the external deficit would have been practically eliminated by 2009, never triggering the liquidity crisis in the Greek economy. The post-2005 deterioration of the external deficit was not induced by the euro, but by the excessive growth of consumption and, more specifically, of public spending, which jumped from €31 billion in 2003 to €62 billion in 2009; (the hike is depicted in Figure 1.3 as a ratio to GDP).

Even if the deterioration of the external deficit had been countered with drastic currency devaluations, the only certain outcome would be the contraction of real wages, not an export-led growth. This is, after all, exactly the legacy of all pre-EMU external devaluations. It is also the experience of the current internal devaluation, through which wages were reduced by 23%, but still export growth remains almost unnoticed.

3.1.5. Greece must follow an economic model different than that of other European economies, because it has a different history and background. Its entry in the single currency acted as a geopolitical 'Procrustean bed', which abolished national idiosyncrasies and enforced integration in many fronts

It is true that the euro is not just a currency, but a passport that grants entry to Europe's core. But this is exactly where Greece historically belongs, and this is where it must stay. Some people may grieve for the fact that Greece was never tied to the apron strings of the United States; others that it didn't become the local ally of the erstwhile USSR or today's Russia; there are even those that mourn because it has never been fully affiliated with authoritarian states such as those of Milosevic's Serbia and communist Bulgaria, or the even more repressive Arab regimes. It is easy to imagine the trouble Greece was spared because none of the above eventualities actually occurred. To avoid any troubles in the future, Greece must remain part of the euro and Europe's core. All else is either ideological obsession, or ignorance of the risks involved.

3.1.6. Greece suffers from archaic administration and chronic institutional shortcomings, which make it impossible to survive in a modern European environment; therefore, it should never have joined the euro

True, several functions of the Greek state are plagued by serious problems; however, any change that was brought about by the euro was for the better, not for the worse. Although in institutional terms, Greece still lags behind several developed countries, there is no doubt that euro membership facilitated—and frequently necessitated—the adoption of crucial reforms to improve transparency and efficiency. These steps would not have been taken outside the euro, simply because the existence of an independent currency enables corporatist interests and business lobbies to exert greater pressures, since they know that the country can always resort to the tactical move of money creation and currency devaluation. The overall lesson is that when an economy is susceptible to pressures, suffers from lack of competition, has inflexible institutions and, in general, shows structural deficiencies, it is in even greater need of a stable and credible currency, so as to act as an anchor of stability and pass the need of reforms in the rest of the economy. Membership in a family of developed countries helps a nation speed up its own adjustment and improvement.

The most commonly cited example of institutional malaise in Greece is corruption. In the past few years, the public debate has been dominated by the exposure of major economic scandals, which involved politicians and senior government officials. The public is infuriated by these phenomena not only on moral grounds, but also because it believes that these scandals put a strain on the economy, thus precipitating the crisis and undermining the efforts to effectively deal with it.

Quite often, the citizens' wrath reaches far beyond the main perpetrators and their political accessories and embraces whole political entities and institutions. Although collective morality is an impracticable concept in Western democracies and each person must be judged on the basis of their own personal actions and decisions, the blame is cast on the entire political system. The sweeping condemnation does not stop even there. Given that many scandals occurred either in the run-up to Greece's accession to the European Monetary Union or in the period that followed it, the drachma evangelists tried to present these instances of corruption as side-effects of the euro's introduction.[2] They secretly reckoned that the citizens' indignation for the squandering of public money and the ethical revolt against the country's ill repute would be transformed into a cathartic movement in favour of exiting the euro. By the same illusion, the new currency they pledge is hoped to be a sort of Chinese wall, insulating the country from corruption.

None of the above could be farther from truth. Greece's Eurozone membership is translated into more—not fewer—means for fighting corruption: from the stricter auditing of the financial system, the taxation of offshore companies and the recourse to EU's anti-corruption structures, to the prevention of speculative attacks against the currency, which, in the past, had been the object of insider dealings and profitable corruption.

By taking part in the process of European integration, Greece not only was compelled to adopt increased transparency in financial administration but was also vested with a much better institutional framework for fighting lawlessness. An exit from the euro will neither hurt those who misappropriated public money, nor trigger a catharsis of the domestic political life. A retrospect of the frequent and long-lasting financial scandals that were dominating public life in the drachma era would be very instructive.

3.1.7. Joining the euro, the Greek economy was deprived of a key development tool and became more susceptible to the pressures of globalization

Exactly because of its susceptibility to multiple external pressures and uncertainties, Greece has since centuries earlier enjoyed lasting economic progress only as long as she was part of stable exchange rate systems, such as:

- The Latin Monetary Union in the last part of the nineteenth century;
- The Gold Standard during the period 1910–1914;
- The interwar Gold Exchange Standard during 1928–1932;
- The post-war currency peg to the dollar, from 1953 to 1972.

After 1973, when the drachma became an independent currency, Greece was persistently plagued by worsening recession and rising inflation. Even in the aftermath of the 2008 crisis, the euro continues to protect the Greek economy much more than an independent currency would have done. Had Greece stayed with the drachma, it would not have experienced only the recent crisis, but three preceding ones as well: in 2003, with the Iraq war; in 2006, with the emergence of the first financial pressures worldwide; and in 2007, with the onset of the credit crunch.

Nor was the euro the mechanism that plunged Greece into the arena of international competition and global pressure. The consequences of globalization had started being felt by the early 1990s, following the collapse of the Eastern European bloc and the opening of China's economy. The relocation of Greek businesses to neighbouring countries in search of lower labour costs had definitely occurred long before the introduction of the euro, not because of it. What's more, in many instances, Greece's accession to the Eurozone helped it face the pressures of globalization from a more robust position.

The main problem caused by the euro was not about exposing Greece to globalization but in widening the rift with other Eurozone countries, especially the northern ones. The common currency proved unable to keep up with the requirements of a full-fledged economic union, when it failed to cope with the creation of a prolonged competitiveness gap between the countries of the North and those of the Southern part of the Eurozone. This internal rift was instrumental in bringing about the Eurozone crisis, as well as in making it difficult to deal with the problem after the event.

3.2. A COMPARISON WITH NON-EURO EU COUNTRIES

In its most complete form, the proposal regarding a possible Grexit is not just put forward as a means of dealing with the current crisis, but also because it is believed that the adoption of the single currency was never of any benefit to the country. Obviously, it is impossible to know exactly how the Greek economy would have fared outside the euro, given the limitations of counter-factual exercises. What can be done, though, is to compare the key economic developments in Greece after its accession to the EMU to those of European Union member states that remained outside the single currency. These countries include the United Kingdom, Sweden and Denmark, which were EU members before Greece but opted to stay out of EMU, as well as the Czech Republic, Hungary and Poland, which became EU members in 2003 but have not yet joined the euro.

These six countries are much different from each other, but each one has some things in common with Greece. Greece has aligned many of its institutional functions and economic practices to those of the EU's oldest member states, and—at the same time—displays many structures of an emerging economy that still characterize the former Eastern bloc countries. In the previous two decades, the six countries pursued very different policies with regard to managing their national currencies: in the United Kingdom, the pound was freely floating; in Sweden and Denmark, the krona and the krone, respectively, were pegged to the euro; while Hungary's forint, the Czech koruna and the Polish zloty went on roller-coaster rides before settling down to more viable exchange rates. It is not unrealistic to assume that, had the drachma continued to exist after 2001, it would have followed a path similar to these alternatives or a combination of them.

What is more, all countries pursued such policies in order to tame inflation, contain deficits and boost growth, irrespective of whether they were being prepared for joining the euro or not. Once again, it would be reasonable to assume that the performance of the Greek economy would fall among those general lines.

Therefore, it is interesting to compare the actual course of the Greek economy with the overall macroeconomic performance of the six non-euro countries during the period 1990–2013. To avoid econometric complications, one can simply choose the best and worst performances among these six countries for each year. The two contours are then compared to Greece's performance as illustrated in the panels of Figure 3.1 and discussed below.

3.2.1. Real GDP Growth

A GDP index is constructed for each country in constant prices and the evolution of these indices both in the previous as well as in the following decade is examined. Base year is chosen to be 2000, that is, the year of Greece's entry to the EMU. In the early 1990s the Greek economy appears to be stagnant, while the other six economies are declining too. This period coincides with the transition of Eastern European countries following the collapse of communist regimes, as well as the deep recession suffered by the EU countries participating in the Exchange Rate Mechanism (ERM) prior to its demise in 1992–1993.

After that, the Greek economy recovered and, as one can see, her growth matched that of the fastest-growing economies until 2007. Therefore, EMU entry did not curb the country's growth dynamism, at least up to the extent experienced by those European economies that remained outside the euro.

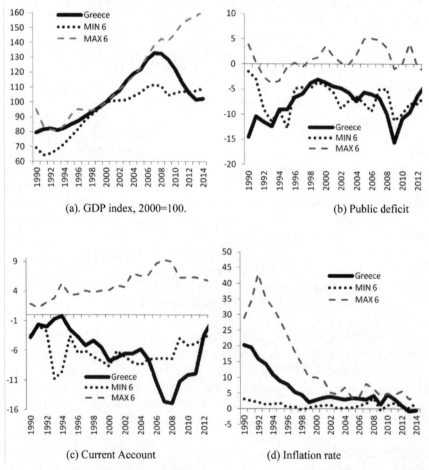

Figure 3.1   Comparing Greece with Other Non-Euro EU Economies. *Source*: Ameco Eurostat. Balnces are percent of GDP.

The Greek economy slowed down in the aftermath of the 2008 crisis, as did other economies as well. But there was a key difference: even slow-growing countries exited recession in 2010, while others (Poland being a case in point) enjoyed a new boost. In contrast, Greece has been suffering even greater contraction as a result of the bailout memorandum, and in 2013 economic activity fell to the level of the year 2000. This contraction has very little to do with the mechanics of Greece's euro membership and a lot more with the deficiencies of the adjustment programme, as will become plain in Part II of the book.

3.2.2. Inflation

In early 1990s, inflation rose in many countries, albeit for very different reasons. In the countries of Eastern Europe, inflation was rampant as a result of violent adjustment of their currencies to the new conditions prevailing in capitalist markets. At the same time, the countries of the European Union were experiencing inflationary pressures following their exit from the ERM. Greece was suffering from double-digit inflation, as a result of huge fiscal deficits and the incessant depreciation of the exchange rate.

After that, all countries, without exception, entered a phase of decelerating inflation, irrespective of whether they looked forward to joining the euro or not. Greece was almost on a median path between the highest and the lowest inflation contours. Therefore, it is obvious that Greece underwent a stabilization process which was, in any case, imperative. If anything, the prospect of EMU membership actually helped the country consolidate this process and render it more reliable.

3.2.3. Public Deficit

In the early 1990s, Greece found itself with outrageous fiscal deficits, and attempted to contain them even before setting EMU entry. All countries had adopted similar fiscal consolidation policies, and Greece's effort was nothing more than a moderate and piecemeal attempt at cleaning its own house.

The global crisis of 2008 caused deficits to rise in all countries, as governments strove to curb the drop in demand. In Greece, though, the exacerbation of the deficit was even more dramatic than in worst-performing non-euro countries, and this is the main reason for the subsequent outbreak of the Greek debt crisis.

3.2.4. External Deficit

The course of the current account deficit is rather revealing. In the early 1990s, one can see an improvement of the Greek external deficit, mainly as a result of the recession that hit the country at that time, as mentioned above. Subsequently, though, the deficit widened after the resumption of growth, then it was somewhat contained by the devaluation of the drachma in 1998, albeit only temporarily. Similar patterns can be seen, for the same reasons, in other economies, despite the fact that they still had the option to devalue.

In the first years after joining the euro, Greece's external deficit improved, demonstrating that the single currency was not by itself the cause of the deficit's exacerbation, as claimed by the opponents of euro membership. This exacerbation occurred after 2005 concomitantly with the fiscal derailment, and both effects led to the emergence of huge twin deficits and the consequent crisis.

***

Summing up, even if Greece had not joined the euro but nevertheless remained in the European Union doing what, more or less, these six countries actually did, there would be no dramatic change in the economic stabilization process. As a matter of fact, the process would be even fiscally tougher, more costly for wage earners and more uncertain for all. The consequences of the smaller crisis preceding 2008 would be larger and the country would have suffered more, without gaining any experience in dealing with an economic shock.

NOTES

1. Data from the IMF database (IMF WEO Database, 2013).
2. Such illogical claims are quite frequently cited in populist media. For example, an analyst in the anti-euro blog 'Drachma' wrote that 'the easy access to international credit at a low interest rate would . . . also broaden the opportunities for bribes, illegal appropriations and kickbacks for the political system'; see http://www.drachmi5.gr/hi-polyhronioy. Reversing the argument, one would hope—against all evidence—that corruption in less developed countries with weaker currencies should be lower than developed ones.

Part II

THE BAILOUT YEARS

Chapter 4

Getting It Wrong

An Appraisal of the Austerity Programme

The main aspects of the bailout agreement are described and the effectiveness of key policy measures regarding revenue collection, competitiveness and privatizations is assessed. On all these fronts, the outcome has been very poor or indeed the opposite of what was intended. Revenues fell despite a substantial rise in tax rates and the imposition of new burdens; privatizations did not materialize despite an ambitious programme of selling public property; exports never took off though private sector wages were severely cut to re-invigorate competitiveness. In the meantime, the economy was hit by a deep recession and high unemployment that subsequently led to social protests and political polarization. The main reasons for the adjustment failures are examined.

4.1. GETTING IT WRONG IN THEORY

In the wake of the 2008 crisis, fiscal deficits started to increase in many countries, either for the purpose of financing the banks' bailouts, or by boosting demand to avert the uncontrollable rise of unemployment, even for providing direct assistance to large enterprises in order to keep them running. But the countries that were already heavily indebted soon ran out of liquidity and faced the dilemma of whether to adopt a fiscal expansion policy and risk further increases in debt or impose austerity measures that would lead to a further contraction of business activity and employment.

To allay such concerns, international organizations and notable academics rushed to produce a theory of fiscal adjustment whereby austerity measures not only ruled out any substantial recessionary risk, but would soon lead to even faster growth, rewarding the governments who implement them in time.

The twin pillars of their austerity optimism were the estimates about the level of optimal debt and the low effect of fiscal multipliers.

4.1.1. Optimal Debt Theories

For many decades, it was taken for granted that fiscal deficits can help boost business activity only if the country has a low level of public debt. In such a case, if the government borrowed to finance infrastructures and other productive activities, future growth would be enhanced, without the markets considering that the country would find it difficult to repay its obligations. In contrast, if debt is already high, any further borrowing will make its repayment more difficult and the markets will 'punish' the government beforehand, by setting interest rates at extremely high levels wiping out any even temporary growth gains. The thesis that a country's excessive debt inevitably leads to economic collapse was commonplace in modern economic thought.

The literature of growth-inducing fiscal consolidation thrived in the early 1990s as European economies cut public debts and deficits on their way toward the EMU.[1] If successful, fiscal consolidation raised the prospects of each particular country joining the EMU and, as a result, ushered in a period of stability, increased capital flows and low interest rates that would spur growth. Anticipating convergence, markets were eager to award the stabilized economies in advance, hence activity was rising as quickly as debt and deficits were being harnessed. The increasing availability of international credit kept world interest rates at low levels, and allowed the convergence game to be successfully played on the way to the creation of the EMU.

As none of these growth-inducing factors was taken for granted after the 2008 crisis, the fiscal impact on growth came under new empirical scrutiny. According to the new theories, debt-augmenting policies (used, e.g. to build infrastructure or to upgrade human capital) could still enhance growth but only until a debt threshold is reached. If exceeded, debt accumulation becomes detrimental to growth and the reverse process is put in motion: cutting debt through larger primary surpluses pushes growth upwards and the debt burden is further relieved from the snowball effects and this generates even more growth. The new and really interesting point, though, was not to be found in the reiteration of a well-known theory, but in the question of what exactly constitutes an 'excessive debt' and whether its threshold varies in periods of economic crisis.

With such a question in mind, two renowned American economists—Kenneth Rogoff and Carmen Reinhart—performed simple correlation tests between growth rates and various sub-samples of debt zones over the period 1946–2009 across both advanced countries and emerging markets. Their conclusion was that high debt/GDP levels of 80% or above are associated with notably lower growth outcomes.[2] Though the study was discovered to contain several factual errors and omissions to the point that—if taken into account—their conclusions are completely invalidated, the austerity-prone message was not apprehended.[3]

In the same vein, a study by the OECD investigated eighteen countries from 1980 to 2010 and concluded that beyond a level of around 85% of GDP, public debt becomes a drag on growth, thus countries in such conditions should act quickly and decisively to address their fiscal woes.[4] This study was followed by many others prepared by the IMF and the ECB, which corroborated the initial finding. A large number of advanced economies were investigated over the period 1970–2007 by an IMF study that also established an inverse relationship between initial debt and subsequent growth: on average, a 10-percentage point increase in the initial debt-to-GDP ratio is associated with a growth slowdown of around 0.2 percentage points per year.[5] The impact is stronger if debt exceeded a threshold of around 90%. An ECB study for the twelve member states of the Eurozone over the period 1971–2008 found that public debt becomes detrimental to growth above a certain level and government deficits exert a negative impact throughout. Hence they strongly argued '. . . *in favour of swiftly implementing ambitious strategies for debt reduction*'.[6]

4.1.2. Missing the Crisis Factor

As these empirical findings were obtained largely by using data prior to 2008, the above results do not distinguish periods before and after the global crisis. Hence, the general implication remained that reducing public debt would not only relieve stressed economies from the burden of increased service costs but also enhance growth and help exiting the great recession.

Given that by (a perhaps magical) coincidence the public debt of the United States, as well as the average public debt of the Eurozone at that time were near those threshold levels, the implied message was that governments should not consider any further fiscal expansion, in order to avoid fuelling the recession any further! If, on the other hand, they opted for fast-track fiscal adjustment, they would be rewarded and growth rates would soon return. This was the theoretical background of the austerity policies that have prevailed ever since. The United States managed to escape this prescription and all of its recessionary implications, but these theories ensnared Europe in a prolonged recession, which hit business activity even in strong economies.

The aforementioned analyses missed an awkward detail that would soon make all the elaborate calculations fall apart: the *crisis* itself, along with the deep changes it brings about, in both economic models and social behaviours. Keynes—who is usually held in contempt by the mainstream view of fiscal zeal—had warned since 1936 that under conditions of severe income reduction, households spend a proportionately larger portion of their income in order to preserve their living standards.[7] In such an environment, excessive austerity may possibly cause a greater economic downturn than would be the case if the reductions took place during a normal period.[8]

To see how the global crisis might have affected the relation between growth and indebtedness, a simple comparison of the relationship in the Eurozone economies is presented in the two periods. The pre-crisis period 2002–2007 includes the years since the circulation of the common currency, while the post-crisis period is 2008–2013. Greece is kept out of the sample, in order to avoid idiosyncratic effects. The other countries constitute a highly diversified group ranging from minimal-debt cases like the Baltic economies to seriously indebted ones like Italy and Belgium.

Results are shown in Figure 4.1. A strong, negative and statistically significant correlation is found for the pre-crisis period, broadly confirming the aforementioned literature of growth-inducing debt-reduction policies. A possible explanation is that highly indebted countries were subject to the requirements of the Growth and Stability Pact to cut their deficits, therefore domestic demand was restricted leading to lower growth. Or their borrowing costs were higher due to the market risk presented by higher debt, thus negatively affecting investment activity.

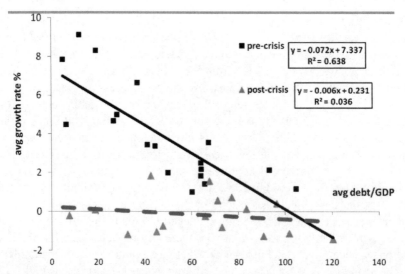

Figure 4.1   Pre- and Post-crisis Growth Rates and Debt Burden in the Eurozone. Eurozone includes all current 19 countries but Greece. Pre-crisis period 2002–2007 (squares, solid regression line). Post-crisis period 2008–2013, (triangles, dotted line). Figures are period averages in percent. *Data source*: IMF WEO Database, October 2014.

Even so, however, the strong correlation does not exactly reflect the causation that is assumed in the debt-cutting theories. According to them, countries with extremely low debt could benefit growth-wise from a fiscal expansion. In fact, the Baltic countries had attained very high growth rates without accumulating debt, simply because they were in the stage of economic transition and rapid capital accumulation.

No element of the Reinhart and Rogoff theory survives in the post-crisis period. The regression line in Figure 4.1 becomes horizontal, implying that correlation is insignificant and growth outcomes cannot be predicted on the basis of indebtedness. Low-debt countries suffered quite a strong recession, while others with higher debt managed to restrain the effects of the crisis. These simple findings are enough to cast serious doubt on the assertion that consolidation is accompanied by a resurgence of growth in the Euro area.

For countries such as Greece, where in 2009 the debt exceeded the 90% threshold by a wide margin, the light-hearted theories presented a convenient alibi for ignoring the risk that a sudden and severe fiscal adjustment would lead to economic collapse. In their self-indulging ignorance of the changes that a crisis brings about in an economy, these theories called for even more urgent action: instead of being gradual, the austerity programmes should be immediate and extensive because, according to the debt-cutting model, this was a safe way that would automatically spur growth.

4.1.3. The Convenient Multipliers

Over the same period, an effort was also undertaken to allay any worries that strict adherence to fiscal adjustment during a crisis would exacerbate, instead of remedying, its consequences. According to official IMF studies that were published in 2010[9], if a country implemented austerity policies the implications would be immaterial and temporary: applying austerity measures equivalent to 1% of GDP would reduce economic activity only by half this percentage, while the increase in unemployment would be negligible, just 0.3% of the labour force. These ratios became known as 'fiscal multipliers', because they estimated the overall effect on an economy from a cut down on expenditure or an increase in taxation.

The small multiplier estimated by the IMF made any recession seem minimal, but even this could be overcome through fast-paced reforms that would bring high growth rates, and this time without excessive debt. This theoretical background was used to justify many things that in retrospect seem strange. Four years after their implementation almost everyone is openly lashing out against the Memorandums, blaming them for causing the recession by being based on erroneous estimates.

The above arguments were not wholly unopposed. An IMF study observed that excessive fiscal zeal might have serious contractionary effects.[10] In other words, the supply-side motives that otherwise would have been invited by redressing public finances, may now be dominated by Keynesian effects. The situation was pointedly described a long time ago by Keynes who argued that in 'abnormal' periods the multiplier is enlarged as 'the propensity to consume may be sharply affected by the development of extreme uncertainty concerning the future and what it may bring forth'.[11]

4.1.4. The Crisis Changed Them All

Whether the global crisis has affected the relation between growth and indebtedness in the Eurozone economies has not been examined in any depth. A slight exception was a study by ECB conceding that after the crisis the permitted ceiling of indebtedness can be extended to 90% of GDP.[12] The idea is that during periods of crisis, a higher debt that is due to temporary fiscal relaxation to support demand may sustain activity and growth, rather than harming them. Or, putting it differently, harsh austerity measures which aim at cutting indebtedness are more likely to generate a severe recession rather than appeal to investors to rush and reward fiscal virtue.

It was not long before that the fundamentalists of growth-inducing austerity came to terms with reality and saw their calculations fail. Although the errors in forecasting Greece's recession were excessive, similar misjudgments are discernible in relation to several other economies undergoing fiscal consolidation. An IMF assessment of twenty eight economies found that the stronger the correction in the fiscal stance, the wider the error in predicting GDP growth, and a similar result is confirmed for the Eurozone economies.[13]

A similar shift in expectation explains the post-crisis change in fiscal multipliers. In the post-crisis period 2008–2012, countries were variably hit by the credit crunch and soon their fiscal stances differed widely. The chief IMF economist admitted that the fiscal multipliers used by IMF authorities to forecast the recessionary impact of debt consolidation programmes in Europe and elsewhere were grossly underestimated, and more likely they were in the range of 0.9 to 1.7 rather than around 0.50 as initially assumed.[14] These findings put an end to the view that austerity would have only mild recessionary effects, and called for revisions of the programmes based on more reliable estimation of the expected multipliers.[15] For the Eurozone in particular, fiscal multipliers in the post-crisis period were estimated and found to be around unity.[16] These findings put an end to the view that austerity would have only mild recessionary effects, and called for revisions of the programmes such as to reflect more reliable estimation of the expected multipliers.

Though indicative, the arguments suggest that the fiscal consolidation programmes applied in the wake of the debt crisis are more likely to have contributed to diminishing growth rates in the Eurozone countries rather than boosting them. Among them, Greece had to apply the most ambitious consolidation programme to reverse the explosive accumulation of public debt. As a consequence she was also hit by a prolonged contraction during the same period.

4.2. GETTING IT WRONG IN PRACTICE

The recession was not forecasted to plumb such depths when the implementation of the first adjustment programme began in May 2010. This early optimism had relied on an Official Report by the IMF in which the growth impact of fiscal consolidation was estimated to be mild and predicted to disappear altogether after two years. Moreover, even these small contractions were expected to be superseded by the growth potential unleashed by rapidly implementing market reforms. At that time, all authorities involved in the austerity programme seemed to be convinced that the deflationary impact would be limited: recession was expected to bottom-out in late 2010 and growth to gradually rebound thereafter.[17]

But, in practice, the programmes, which took no heed of Keynes's warnings, were soon proved to be fatefully wrong: in all the countries they were implemented, recession estimates missed by a factor of two, while in the case of Greece recession proved to be quadruple than originally forecast. For example, the IMF believed[18] that in the period 2012–2013 the Greek economy would grow by a nominal total rate of 4.3%. In practice, recession was so severe that the cumulative downturn reached −12%. In other words, the error amounted to more than 16% of GDP just for this specific two-year period.

The forecasts made by other parties were wildly far from the mark as well. Figure 4.2 shows the continuous updating of projections for the cumulative real growth expected for Greece over the period 2012–2013. From a hopeful forecasting of positive real growth by +3.2% a few months after the implementation of the programme, predictions were adjusted to an alarming downturn by −4.7% in early 2012, only to be superseded by the dismal −11.5% by which the economy actually contracted.

The reasons why such serious forecasting errors went unnoticed are, nonetheless, different for each party that was involved in Greece's programme. The IMF implements standard prescriptions in all countries, without having any feedback rules for early correction in case things go wrong. The Eurozone ignored the issue altogether and did not wish to respond to the problem that some of its members were facing, by acting as a single economic space.

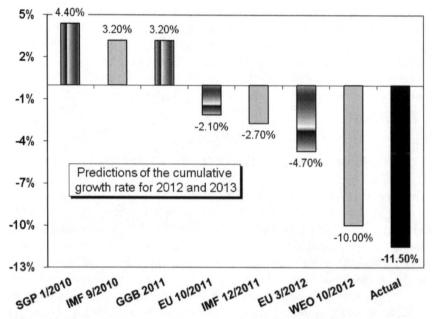

Figure 4.2 Updating Projections: From Optimism to Harsh Reality. *Sources*: Greek Government forecasts are denoted by vertical pattern and come from: Stability & Growth Plan, Fin Min Greece, 01/01/2010, p. 16. Budget report for 2011, 01/11/2010, p. 24. IMF's by solid grey from: IMF Country Report No. 10/286, 01/09/2010, p. 26. No. 11/351, 01/12/2011, p. 53. WEO October 2012. EU's by horizontal pattern from: European Economy No 87, 01/10/2011, p. 14. No 94, 01/3/2012, p. 140. Actual data in solid black from: Ameco Eurostat.

Even the OECD noted in 2014 the institutional and political unpreparedness of the Eurozone. In the report, the assertion that front-loaded fiscal adjustment is always a necessary response was met with a scalding criticism that the policy 'consigned millions to unemployment and poverty'. Responding to the assertion by the IMF that all organizations had made errors in their calculations of fiscal multipliers, the OECD accused the Eurozone of erring dramatically in its expectation that the crisis would soon subside without any need to change intervention mechanisms.[19]

4.3. SHORTCOMINGS OF THE GREEK STABILIZATION

The adjustment programme for Greece involved extensive and universal cuts in expenditure, several tax hikes on households and property and an ambitious plan of market reforms and privatizations to attract new investments and promote growth. During this process, too many things went wrong and, far from containing fiscal imbalances in time, most targets were missed and the debt burden continued to rise. Though some reform initiatives applied in the social security system, the health sector and in budgetary procedures were in the right direction and had some impact in containing the deficit, others failed. For example, attempts at liberalizing the vocational licensing system in various sectors failed to spur any growth as recession was effectively inhibiting potential new entrants. In reforming public entities or privatization plans, the failure was more extensive in spite of expensive preparations and political costs.

Ignoring the warnings that deep cuts in incomes would lead to deep recession, authorities added salt to the wound by adopting positive feedback tactics: whenever a fiscal target was missed, measures—rather than being re-examined—were intensified in the same direction. Such tactics further exhausted the disposable incomes of households and—at the same time—had detrimental effects on revenues.

4.3.1. No Rise in Exports

A welcome development was the containment of the current account deficit from a horrendous 15% of GDP in 2009 to less than 6% of GDP by the end of 2012.[20] But even this was hardly a cause for celebration, as the main reason was that imports had shrunk due to the curtailment of demand and only a small fraction is attributable to improvements in competitiveness. Average wages in the private sector had been cut by 22%, leading to impressive reductions of unit labour costs.[21] All deterioration that had occurred during the EMU period vanished overnight, and the relevant productivity index returned to the 2000 level.[22] However, Greek firms suffering from lack of liquidity were not in a position to take advantage of the situation and the index of real effective exchange rate improved only marginally by 2.8% in 2012 relative to 2009. Non-oil exports increased by just 1.42% in 2012, year-on-year. They remained even inferior to the rise in world demand of goods and services by 3.2% over the same period,[23] as the exportability of Greek production has not been seriously improved.[24]

4.3.2. Tax Rhetoric Without Revenues

With a dithering record on tax collection, the government finally rushed in March 2010 to quickly raise more revenues by increasing the VAT rate from 19% to 21%.[25] Although experience from a similar decision to raise the VAT rate by 1% in 2005 suggested that it is more likely to be pocketed by retailers as an excuse to increase prices, instead of boosting tax revenues, the authorities were hoping that recession would this time negate the effect of inflation. To buttress against increased incentives for VAT appropriation by retailers, the government launched a campaign to induce receipt-collection and announced further measures to beat tax evasion.

With no evidence of success in the first two months, a similar measure was recommended by the Memorandum. In May 2010, the VAT rate was raised again to 23% and calculations proved, once more, to be unrealistic. Amid recession, CPI inflation was rampaging at 4.5% at the end of 2010, substantially above the previous years. With growth plummeting, the economy ended up in a typical stagflation trap, fiscal revenues did not improve and debt continued to rapidly accumulate.[26]

Although revenues were additionally enhanced by a lucrative lump-sum tax in exchange for settling previous arrears *('peraiosis')*, a heavy increase in fuel tax, and a substantial rise in several consumption surcharges, net collection remained virtually the same as in the corresponding months before the tax storm. Since nominal GDP remained roughly the same between 2009 and 2010, the failure to raise revenues should be attributed solely to the continuing slackness in the collection mechanism and the increased incentives for evading it. Despite the increased tax burden, income tax revenues—as a result of either recession or increased evasion—declined substantially even in comparison to the slack year 2009, as most tax increases fell upon personal income while the business sector was left unaffected so as to avoid a further slump; the tax burden on households relative to the corporate sector increased twofold between 2009 and 2013.

The same effect of increasing rates and falling revenues was experienced in indirect taxation. The VAT rate increased from 18% in 2009 to 23% in 2012, but revenues were constantly falling due to reduced purchasing power. Figure 4.3 displays the inverse relation between rising rates and falling revenues that frustrated tax authorities. In spite of several warnings that the key to raise revenues is not raising the marginal rates but extending the tax base and strengthening auditing to beat evasion, the authorities kept insisting on

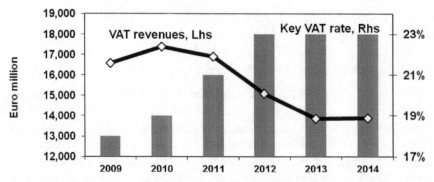

Figure 4.3   Key Rates of, and Revenues From, VAT. *Source*: Budget Report, various issues. Ministry of Finance, Greece.

the same recipe leading to further recession.[27] With a lax auditing regime, liquidity-starving retailers quickly recognized that the VAT increase presented them with a new opportunity for cashing the tax, which was worth enough to ignore the little risk of apprehension.

4.3.3. Failing to Collect

Immediately after the signing of the austerity programme, the government agreed to introduce several wage cuts in the public sector and also to reduce pensions in all Social Security Funds. Actual implementation, however, was a different story. The government faced a war of attrition by the trade unions in the public sector, and was also greatly embarrassed by its own ranks, which mainly consisted of public employees. The result was that several of the measures were either postponed or diluted: at the end of the year, the government had paid a highly damaging political cost for initiating the austerity measures, but without securing any substantial fiscal gain.

Figure 4.4 illustrates this embarrassing reality by comparing the 2010 average income as declared by wagers and pensioners in their 2011 tax statements. Despite the presumed cuts, average wages did actually fall during 2010 by only -2.65% and pensions by less than 1% relative to 2009.

The comparison with the average incomes in the crisis year 2008 is even more revealing. Two years after the global crisis, the average public wage was roughly the same, while pensions had in fact risen by +3.40% on average.

The most disturbing collapse, however, was that of income tax revenues and shows how well-intentioned but nevertheless ill-prepared policies lead

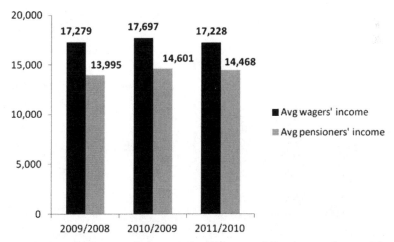

Figure 4.4 Average Income Statements by Wagers and Pensioners. *Source*: Min. of Finance, General Secretary of Information System. http://www.gsis.gr/gsis/info/gsis_site/PublicIssue/Statistics.html.

to opposite results. The government had vowed to beat tax evasion and raise the number of households liable to submit tax returns. A large-scale media campaign was orchestrated and public opinion was bombarded with numerous revelations of tax dodgers and punitive plans to enforce tax law. But at the end, the government failed to mobilize the revenue collection mechanism or increase auditing to crack down on VAT evasion by retail firms and professionals. Despite the costly media campaign, tax compliance was in fact diminished in 2010! The tax returns submitted in 2011 for the previous fiscal year were reduced by 13,192—fewer even relative to 2009, a year that was rightly regarded as a singularly lax period due to the two elections and the general climate of complacency and abandonment.

The failure to expand VAT revenues spread panic and led to such poorly prepared improvisations that further aggravated the problem. As the withholding of VAT payments by retailers is a major source of tax evasion in Greece, the government introduced the measure of receipt collection as an incentive to customers for demanding a registered transaction. In return, receipts would be submitted with tax returns and raise the untaxed threshold. The measure could have worked if eligible receipts had been solely obtained from the main evasion-prone sectors, such as tourism, housing services, medics, etc. But in the absence of any criterion, the option turned into a massive tax deduction facility for ordinary households. Early calculations proved to be grossly misleading, and the measure led to vast amounts of income being excluded from taxation.

The onerous result is displayed in Figure 4.5. The average tax paid per household for the fiscal year 2010 fell by −18.61% relative to the previous

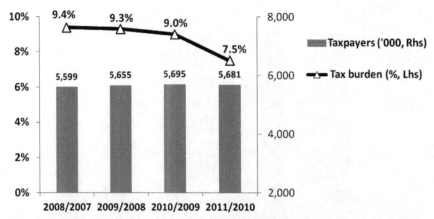

Figure 4.5 The Collapse of Income Tax Revenues in 2011. *Notes:* Average declared income is obtained by total divided by the number of taxpayers. Tax burden is the ratio of tax to declared income, in percent. *Source:* Min. of Finance, General Secretary of Information System. http://www.gsis.gr/gsis/info/gsis_site/

year. Even if the contraction of average income by −2.30% is taken into account, the end result is a net cut in income tax by more than 16%. In combination with the small reduction in nominal incomes, this led to keeping disposable incomes almost intact on average (a reduction of just ½ percent is calculated from the data).

Though unintentional, that was, perhaps, the largest tax boost observed in a single year in any European state in the post-war period. The fact that such a major tax relief unintentionally took place in a country deep in a debt crisis and already bailed-out is one of the biggest ironies in the five-year saga of the austerity programme. Under different circumstances, this outcome could be perceived as blatant Keynesianism perfectly designed to sustain demand and thwart any looming recession away. But it didn't happen this time. Panicked by the collapse in revenues, the government conceded to a new series of tax rises and further austerity.

4.4. FROM UNWILLINGNESS TO MISFIRE

The Greek government accepted the IMF framework without any preparation for its consequences or any comprehensive planning for its implementation. Perhaps the ruling party viewed the IMF's involvement as politically convenient, believing that it could blame the Fund for the imposition of unpleasant measures which the government was in no position to enact on its own. The assumption that the crisis could be dealt with in only one year made the acceptance of the programme seem like a brief interlude and everyone expected that the country would soon return to business-as-usual. Soon, everything would be on a fast-track again. The true outcome disproved such light-hearted calculations just after the first year of implementation. A brief assessment is given below.

4.4.1. Reforms Without Growth

The bailout Memorandum included the implementation of structural reforms that would reduce various scleroses in the economy, cut red-tape practices in entrepreneurship, shrink public ownership in utilities and ultimately improve competitiveness. Such reforms were seen as sufficient to harness recession and bring about growth without applying Keynesian recipes to the overstretched deficits.

In practice, however, success has been limited and in any case far from generating any growth at all. A major reform took place in the ailing social security system, raising age limits, extending backwards the salary base on which pensions are calculated and rationalizing the overly abused provisions for early retirements. Even this reform, however, did not have any immediate fiscal benefit as savings will mostly occur in the future. Ironically, several pension funds were further burdened by the rush of near-retirement employees—mainly in the public sector—to take advantage of favourable transition clauses and exit service before the new regime was applied.

Ending barriers to entry in a number of activities was fiercely opposed by the insiders and the initial plans were seriously compromised. For example, liberalization of lorry licensing was granted a postponement for two years, while the lifting of downward price controls in lawyers and dispensing chemists was watered-down to the point of no real effect. Not surprisingly, these reforms were not exchanged for more growth and, without any other supply or demand-driven initiative in sight, the economy experienced deeper recession in 2010 and even more afterwards.

4.4.2. Lower Public Consumption, but No Privatizations

The first Memorandum was more successful in curtailing the explosive path of public consumption from €62.3 billion in 2009 down to €55.6 billion in 2010, through universal pension and salary cuts. That was the main reason for bringing the general government deficit from the ominous 15.4% of GDP in 2009 to around 10.40% of GDP in 2010. Given the strong affiliation of public unions to the ruling party, the implementation of expenditure cuts involved a high political cost for the government to a degree that further measures of the same kind are unlikely.

4.4.3. A Last-ditch Attempt: Fast-track Privatizations

On the other hand, the more promising front of privatizations remained completely inactive, until decisions to speed them up were finally taken in mid-2011. Although the dynamics of the debt-to-GDP ratio are sensitive to the prospects of growth, no explicit action was considered to improve it. In 2011, the debt was expected to escalate above 156% of GDP before starting to slowly decline after 2014. Frightened by such a bleak prospect, the government succumbed to pressures from the IMF and European Union institutions, and half-heartedly announced an ambitious programme that included extensive privatizations of public companies and a plan for the development of real-estate on public property.[28] The programme aimed at collecting proceeds of €50 billion during the period 2011–2015, or roughly 4% of GDP per annum in average. The proceeds of the programme would be earmarked for buying back debt.

Despite the strong rhetoric, this target was quickly abandoned for two reasons: First because, as history suggests, privatizations have seldom been popular in Greece and it was only in the run-up to EMU that the government decided to invite private investors to participate in the ownership of state-owned companies. Even at that time, however, proceeds never exceeded 2% of GDP, though there was no way to do it when markets were collapsing. The second reason is that although privatizations were mostly neglected in the preceding years, and for the programme to be put again in motion an extensive and careful planning was required, the mechanisms were not in place to carry the plan through.

4.5. PUNISHMENT OR PENITENCE

When the first Memorandum was launched, many people seemed content and unconcerned about the consequences. The leaderships of the Eurozone believed that they had done away with the Greek problem, by allocating all supervising responsibilities to the IMF. It is fair to recall at this point that the EU had left the problem to grow to gigantic proportions by exercising no control over the actions of the Greek governments during the period 2007–2009, when thousands of people were being hired in the public sector and state revenues were tumbling. By insisting on the IMF's participation in the supervision of the Memorandum, they would somehow manage to hide their own unpreparedness, while the Fund's harsh prescriptions would also act as a kind of punishment for the delinquent country. Thus, Europe was divided into 'virtuous' and 'prodigal' countries, whose punishment would set an example for the others.

4.5.1. Purgatorial Economics

It is often argued that austerity programmes are necessary not only for redressing public finances in a country but also for subsequently fostering a culture of prudence in society. In this way, malpractices were cut, and more efficient and ethical procedures in economic and social activity were adopted. According to such fiscal zealots, Greece deserved to suffer the shortcomings of the adjustment programme as a means to pay a price for past profligacy. No less than Timothy Geithner, then US Secretary of the Treasury, was astonished to discover that several Eurozone countries viewed harsh austerity as a rightful punishment for the sinful Greece. Recalling an emergency meeting in 2011 over the Eurozone crisis, Geithner recalled that:[29]

> the Europeans came into that meeting basically saying: *'We're going to teach the Greeks a lesson. They are really terrible. They lied to us. They suck and they were profligate and took advantage of the whole basic thing and we're going to crush them'*, was their basic attitude, all of them.

As the austerity programme proved to be notoriously ineffective in getting the economy out of the crisis, it is perhaps tempting to see whether it was at least capable for delivering the moral lesson to Greece. The Worldwide Governance Indicators published by the World Bank are used as proxies for how the above factors evolved from 1996 to 2013; see Figure 4.6.

The average score in the pre-crisis years is then compared with the score during the crisis 2009–2013 in Table 4.1. It is striking that all good governance indicators deteriorate in the post-crisis period. Accountability indicators waned because several of the austerity measures were enacted with insufficient consultation in Parliament, and, in some key decisions, as mere cabinet acts.

Political stability was shaken as many MPs deserted their parties, and society was torn apart by violent demonstrations and clashes. This hit government effectiveness and cohesion severely. It is perhaps telling that during the period under review (2009–2014), there have been seven different ministers of Finance, some of them serving for just a few months. Corruption increased and the rule of law weakened as economic conditions deteriorated, social deprivation was spreading and public trust was discredited. It is only regarding the regulatory environment that the decline is small, due to some reforms that were implemented as part of the austerity programme. But even these

Figure 4.6 World Bank Governance Indicators. *Source*: World Bank, Country Report for Greece, 1996–2013.

Table 4.1 Comparing Pre-crisis and Post-crisis Indicators

Index, Original Data	Pre-crisis Average 1996–2008	Post-crisis Average 2009–2013	Change in Percent
Voice and Accountability	79.00	70.58	–11%
Political Stability and Absence of Violence	64.02	39.92	–38%
Government Effectiveness	74.71	67.72	–9%
Regulatory Quality	76.32	71.92	–6%
Rule of Law	74.63	65.64	–12%
Control of Corruption	69.80	55.16	–21%
Ranking by the Global Competitiveness Index	**46**	**86**	**worse by 87%**

Note: Figures are period averages.
Source: As in Figure 1.6.

did not exert any noticeable effect in correcting the economy and boosting business activity.

4.5.2. Institutional and Political Failures

However critical the consequences might have been, the omission to account for the higher multipliers was not the only mischief. Even more serious costs were brought about by ignoring what two Nobel Prize winners—George Akerlof and Robert Shiller—aptly coined as the *'confidence multiplier'*, a factor affecting social and political behaviour in a way that the crisis is further propagated rather than restrained.[30]

In the wake of the debt crisis, Greece suffered from a systemic threat that the country may be forced to abandon the Eurozone, an event that would inflict major capital losses on euro-denominated deposits. Capital flight ensued, further damaging domestic liquidity and accelerating fears that the economy might collapse. Public opinion was losing confidence that authorities could drive the economy out of the crisis in a reasonable time-window and this had two serious consequences: first, it undermined the efficacy of measures as private market players adjusted their expectations that stabilization will take much longer than envisaged, thus postponing or cancelling medium-term plans for new investment in Greece; second, it made vested interest opposition to the conditionality programme widespread and protracted, thus raising the social and political cost of implementing reforms to prohibitive levels.

The political and institutional fallout was significant even since 2011, just one year after the implementation of the austerity programme. Mainstream parties saw their influence shrink at less than half of the pre-crisis levels, while a radical polarization emerged on both ends of the political spectrum. On top of chronic deficiencies, institutions crumbled too, both as a result of overload due to mounting numbers of economic and social disputes and because of low motivation and job shirking as a reaction to deep wage cuts in the public sector.

It is interesting to examine how the loss of confidence affected the image of Greece as an attractive investment destination. Using the popular indicator of outwardly competitiveness composed annually by the World Economic Forum (2012), Greece continued to decline and ranked 96th among 144 countries. This implies a loss of 25 positions relative to 2009, that is, the year before the conditionality programme was launched.

Naturally, the main drive of such deterioration was the country's macroeconomic instability, which stemmed from the debt crisis and the risk of collapse and exiting the Eurozone. But equally telling is the abysmal record of institutional capacity which fell to the 111th place, a retreat by 40 positions relative to 2009.[31] On the other hand, physical infrastructures remained relatively unscathed, though persisting under-financing for maintenance costs due to the fiscal cuts may soon take its toll in this sector as well.

***

The front-loaded character of the austerity programme in Greece was ill-suited to stave off recession. As the recession worsened, the targets set by the programme were serially missed, inviting a new round of similar actions with the same predictable contraction. The economy notwithstanding, Greece suffered a backlash on many institutional, social and value issues. Perhaps the greatest irony was that, although the programme was conceived as a response to a looming public debt and to stagnant production, the outcome was even more bizarre: public debt rose enormously relative to the levels at the beginning of the crisis, while disinvestment was so extensive that a substantial part of the productive capacity was destroyed.

NOTES

1. Among many others, Giavazzi and Pagano (1990 and 1996), Alesina and Perotti (1997), Alesina and Ardagna (1998). For the case of Greece, see Christodoulakis (1994).

2. See Reinhart and Rogoff (2010).

3. The demolition of the Reinhart and Rogoff thesis was dealt with by Herndon et al. (2013). For a non-technical discussion of the issue, see Cassidy (2013).

4. Cecchetti et al. (2011).

5. Kumar and Woo (2010).

6. Checcherita and Rother (2010).

7. Keynes (1936).

8. More recent studies estimated fiscal multipliers at much higher levels. See, for example, Blanchard and Leigh, (2013). For Europe, fiscal multipliers were estimated at 1.20–1.50; see Christodoulakis (2013a).

9. WEO, 2010.

10. Cottarelli and Jaramillo (2012)

11. Keynes (1936, p. 125).

12. See for example, Checherita and Rother (2010), 'The impact of high and growing government debt on economic growth: an empirical investigation for the Eurozone'. The IMF published the paper by Kumar and Woo (2010), 'Public Debt and Growth'. The threshold was extended to 90% by a later study by Baum, Checherita and Rother (2012), 'Debt and growth: new evidence for the Eurozone'.

13. See WEO (2012, Box 1.1) and EC (2012c, pp. 42–43), respectively.

14. See Blanchard and Leigh (2013).

15. The Greek government already raised the issue of a possible re-assessment of the Adjustment Programme in the Eurogroup meeting of February 11, 2013.

16. See Blanchard and Leigh (2013).

17. Data from WEO (2012, p. 165).

18. IMF Report, September 2010, p. 26.

19. The statement by Pier Carlo Padoan, chief economist at the OECD, and the arguments used by IMF are reported in the *Financial Times*, 11/2/2014. http://www.ft.com/intl/cms/s/0/a4b1e3aa-9320-11e3-8ea7-00144feab7de.html#axzz3YaoDBT5G.

20. IMF WEO Database, October 2012.

21. The minimum salary in 2011 was at €746 per month and was cut to €603 in 2012 and then to €586 in 2011. Data from Bank of Greece, Conjectural economic indicators, Table III.3, p. 76.

22. See ECB, Harmonized competitiveness indicators based on unit labour costs indices for the total economy (1999Q1=100). In 2012Q2 the index was 89, exactly the same as the 2000 average.

23. IMF, Ibid.

24. Calculations are by the author based on data from Bank of Greece, Conjectural economic indicators, Table VI.7, p. 146.

25. In an interesting comparison, the British government, responding to a similar pressure of post-crisis recession and looming deficits, decided to reduce the VAT rate by two percentage points.

26. Mabbet and Schelkle (2010) timely pointed out that 'forcing the besieged state to fiscal contraction makes it so much harder, if not impossible to get back on a sustainable path'.

27. Another vivid manifestation of Laffer-curve effects took place in autumn 2012 when the levy on heating fuel was increased from €60 to €330 per metric ton, more than fivefold. With a seasonal consumption of around 4 million tons, the government expected to raise more than €1 billion in extra revenues. The actual outcome showed a poor increase of only €30 million, as fuel demand dropped and households shifted to alternative supplies.

28. The same plan was announced by IMF–EU–ECB representatives in February 2011, but it was fiercely rejected by the government. Later, the government adopted a more flexible line before finally accepting the initial plan.

29. Quoted by Peter Spiegel in the *Financial Times*, 11 Nov. 2014. http://blogs. ft.com/brusselsblog/2014/11/11/draghis-ecb-management-the-leaked-geithner-files/. More details are in Geithner 2014.

30. Akerlof and Shiller (2009).

31. Rankings are taken from the same source as in Figure 1.6: reports.weforum. org/global-competitiveness-report-2014-2015/rankings

Chapter 5

The Vicious Circle

Snowballs, Haircuts and Hazards

One of the grand failures of the austerity programme was the inability to reduce the debt burden, the extent of which was supposed to be the reason for orchestrating the bailout agreement in the first place. The so-called 'snowball effect' is examined in detail and it is shown that lack of growth makes debt even less sustainable, in spite of intense fiscal measures to harness public deficits. It also describes the private sector involvement (PSI) scheme that took place in 2012 and explains why it failed to stabilize debt.

The most problematic characteristic of the recession in Greece has been the massive fall in overall investment activity and the accompanying explosion of unemployment as discussed in this chapter.

5.1. WHY DEBT CONTINUES TO RISE

The increase of a country's debt as a percentage of GDP may be due to three reasons: the creation of a primary deficit, which is added each year to debt; the increase in borrowing costs that put a charge on debt servicing; and the contraction of GDP, which reduces the denominator of the debt burden ratio. The debt burden can be reduced when the above factors are reversed or, otherwise, a direct cut in obligations is applied. The latter was applied in 2012 through the PSI scheme (a procedure that introduced the mandatory participation of private investors in the debt 'haircut'). The idea of private sector involvement originated from Germany and eventually was imposed on all banks and investment funds—domestic and foreign—compelling them to accept part of the cost of the adjustment as a penalty for being too eager to lend to deficit-prone economies. It is interesting to examine how all these factors and actions actually impacted on the Greek debt after the crisis.

When Greece entered the bailout, the austerity programme sought to put a check on the first factor, that is, the deficit, while the loans extended to the country by the bailout agreement helped contain the second one, that is, the cost of borrowing. The third factor proved to be more painful and failed completely. Greece in 2013 and 2014 eventually managed to reverse the negative image of its twin deficits, which were considered to be responsible for the crisis and necessitated the introduction of the Memorandum. At the same time, other variables improved as well: labour-cost competitiveness was restored to 2000 levels, while borrowing spreads were substantially reduced, enabling the country to make a re-entry to the bond market in 2014—albeit brief.

However, the third factor, that of a prolonged recession, was completely ignored and sparked the rapid deterioration of debt, despite the measures taken for dealing with the other two. This is the so-called 'snowball effect on debt', the extent of which depends on the size of the debt.[1] Higher-indebted countries suffer a stronger snowball effect and this may lead to a self-perpetuating rise. The effect is shown in Figure 5.1. For the Eurozone as a whole, the effect peaked only in 2009, as a result of rising borrowing costs and the post-crisis slump.[2] In Greece, however, the 'snowball' effect went on the rise, augmenting debt by as much as 17% of GDP per year. As a result, fiscal consolidation that was initially necessitated by the explosive debt was fuelling such a recession that made the very same debt seem even more explosive afterwards.

In order to assess the true effect of the PSI, the debt trajectory that would prevail in its absence should be constructed. Assuming that nominal GDP

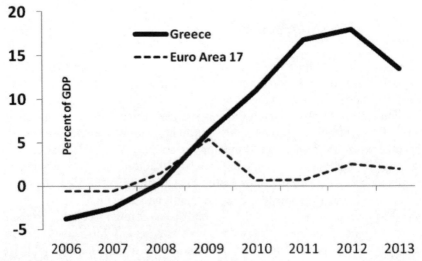

Figure 5.1 The Snowball Effect in Greece and the Euro Area. *Source*: Ameco Eurostat. Data are percent of GDP.

and deficits would be the same without the PSI, the counterfactual path is calculated and shown in Figure 5.2. Results reveal that the true improvement brought about by the PSI was to the tune of 25% of GDP.

Similarly, to understand the effect of recession on a heavily indebted economy, one can estimate the level of debt under the counterfactual assumption that there was no recession. Let's hypothesize that in 2009–2013 the Greek economy had faced a mild recession of approximately –2% per year, like the other countries of the European periphery. Given an average inflation of 2%, this would mean that nominal GDP would have roughly remained stagnant at the 2008 levels. This differential would be enough to bring the debt to 157% of GDP in 2014 without any 'haircut' in between. In other words, the debt would be 22% of GDP lower than the one that was left after the PSI.

5.2. THE LIMITS OF PSI

Despite the significant reductions that were seemingly effected by the PSI, indebtedness had only a brief respite in 2012 and then kept on increasing again, and we need to understand the profound cause of this ensnarement. Apart from the impact of recession through the snowball effect, the unstoppable rise of the debt burden was fuelled by the particular method chosen for reducing the debt. In general, the scheme did lead to the reduction of future

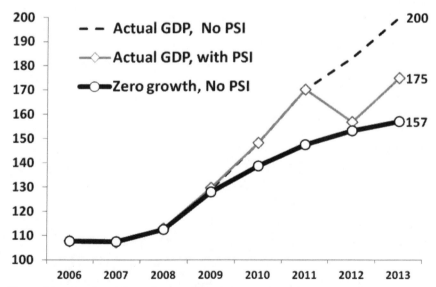

Figure 5.2 Greek Public Debt, Actual and Counterfactuals. (a): Actual GDP, no PSI effect. (b): Actual debt. (c): Assuming constant nominal GDP and no PSI effect. *Source:* Ameco Eurostat. Data are percent of GDP.

claims by foreign banks that had extended loans to the Greek state, as well as by many foreign investment funds that had invested in Greek government bonds. However, when the scheme was applied to Greek banks and social security funds, it led to several mishaps that substantially reduced its effect. The Bank of Greece estimated that of the amount of €137.9 billion that were nominally removed from the stock of Greek bonds, debt was finally reduced by only €51.5 billion, below half of the endeavour.[3] The key reasons for this poor outcome are the following.

5.2.1. Recapitalization of the Greek Banks.

Greek banks were compelled to participate in the PSI, thus incurring a loss of almost €30 billion and their assets were reduced. Since they are obliged to maintain increased reserves as a hedge against the crisis-augmented subserviced loans, they had to cover this amount through state subsidies, financed through the bailout loans granted to the Greek government through the European Stability Mechanism (ESM). Public debt was increased by an equal amount and any gain from the 'haircut' was fully cancelled. In the meantime, though, this process had imposed a huge cost on the Greek economy by perpetuating uncertainty in the banking system, let alone the expenses related to the countless studies that had to be conducted in order to reach these decisions.

But there was another collateral effect: As the funds for recapitalization were provided by the ESM, they were collateralized with preferential shares of the banks. In this way, the Hellenic Financial Stability Fund (HFSF), which is ESM's branch in Greece, acquired a controlling majority in all systemic banks in Greece adding further bureaucratic impediments and costs. This outcome belies the misguided principles on which PSI was conceived and conducted. Initially, Greek banks were in no serious way exposed by toxic assets save for the massive acquisitions of government bonds. The enforced cut in their value, so as to enable the government to reduce its debt, resulted in losing control that was subsequently resumed by public organizations. Since the management of the HFSF is directly appointed by the government, the latter has been effectively invested with discretionary power over the banking system.

5.2.2. Curtailing the Assets of Social Security Funds

Moreover, the end effect on debt accounting from the 'haircut' on government bonds held by social security funds and other public entities (e.g. universities) was also nil. Since these institutions are part of the broader public sector, the government bonds they have acquired are recorded as assets and matched one by one with the corresponding liabilities issued by the central government. No matter if the bonds are accounted for in their full or written-off value, there is no end effect on the final calculation of the general government debt. The only consequence of the PSI was to disrupt the operation of social security funds; moreover, as many of them were since then facing larger deficits, they pressed for additional budget subsidies, thus stretching the cash deficits in a crucial period. Too much ado about nothing!

5.2.3. Squeezing Small Bondholders

The problems caused by the 'haircut' that was imposed on small private bondholders far outweighed any meagre benefits. The PSI scheme punished those individuals who reasonably assumed that placing some of their savings in Greek government debt would be equally as safe as—if not safer than— keeping them in Greek bank deposits which are also guaranteed, up to an amount, by the Greek state. In other times, such bond investment behaviour had been praised as national solidarity, encouraging domestic retail depositors to lend money to the Greek state in periods of pressure.

These people had offered crucial assistance to the Greek economy, whenever liquidity shrank as a result of exogenous or speculative shocks as, for example, during the fiscal crises of 1989, 1994 and 1997. Retail bondholders will not easily trust the Greek state again for many years, forcing it to resort to more costly sources of finance from abroad. If one takes into account the cost stemming from the extra premium that will be paid to foreign creditors, it is highly doubtful whether the government actually gained anything at all from the harsh surprise that it had in store for its most faithful lenders.

5.3. DISINVESTMENT AND UNEMPLOYMENT

5.3.1. The Collapse of the Investment Share

In Greece, total investment suffered a large drop during the years of austerity. The consequences of the debt crisis and the front-loaded fiscal adjustment that followed over the last five years seem to be more ominous and far-reaching than initially expected. Thus far, the country has experienced the deepest recession ever afflicting a European nation in the post-war era: employment in 2014 had decreased by 15%, relative to the levels in 2010, causing extensive social deprivation and political turmoil.[4] An equally threatening—though rarely discussed—consequence of the recession is the massive fall in overall investment activity, which has caused a reduction in net capital stock by 6.3% in real terms relative to its 2010 level, an event unprecedented in non-war times.[5]

The reason why the drop in investment was so extensive is because its share in GDP does not remain unchanged, but is affected by the growth rate. This happens because in periods of recession the adjustment of consumption is not equal to the adjustment of investment. Striving to maintain their living standards, households reduce consumer spending, albeit less than implied by the reduction of their income, and as a result the share of consumer spending in GDP remains almost unchanged, and in some instances even grows.[6] Therefore, the share of capital spending will shrink much more than the share of consumption, leading to a 'double whammy' in regard to investment: initially, the drop of investment is due to economic downturn, but then, as the share of investment expenditure decreases, investment is reduced even further.

The collapse in investment characterizes both the private and the public sector. All investment sectors were severely hit by recession, as shown in Figure 5.3. Two of them, however, collapsed more than others: investment in new dwellings fell to one-tenth of its pre-crisis peak after the burst of the real-estate bubble, while investment in equipment fell to around one-third of that. Non-residential construction was the most resistant, and this is partly due to the public investment component that was partially recovered due to higher utilization of the funds from the Community Support Framework (CSF).

Disinvestment takes an even more dramatic look if capital formation net of replenishment investment is considered. From €56 billion, the sum of new investment and replacement of existing stock fell to €24 billion in 2013. This amounts to a drop of −57%, much larger than the contraction of economic activity. As a share to output, fixed investment added to the capital stock each

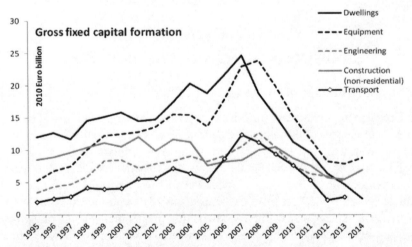

Figure 5.3 The Fall of Investment in Greece, by Sector of Activity. In 2010 constant prices, Euro billion. *Source:* Ameco Eurostat. The Engineering sector is the sum of investment in machinery and metals.

year before the crisis was around 12–15% of GDP. Since then it has fallen abysmally to –10% of GDP in 2013 and 2014. In other words, the physical capital in Greece is being disinvested by the year, and its restoration will require a major investment effort.

5.3.2. The Mirror Evil

The steep fall in investment is mirrored by a steep rise in unemployment. Figure 5.4 shows that gross fixed capital formation in Greece had collapsed to 13% of GDP, below half the level before the crisis, while unemployment followed a symmetric explosion: it is currently running at around 25% of the workforce, more than three times higher than pre-crisis levels.

Though the fall of investment in Greece is the most extensive, underinvestment is also common in other Eurozone countries, causing recovery to be slow and unemployment to run high. No wonder then that, more recently, academic and policy attention has started focusing on the need to accelerate investment activity as the key to exiting recession and creating jobs. A study published by the European Investment Bank (EIB) admitted that the EU is hit by 'a historically unprecedented collapse in fixed capital formation' and described a priority list—from the acceleration of reforms to industrial restructuring to financial support—to mitigate its impact.[7]

The debate becomes more relevant in the light of a major initiative recently approved by the European Commission. The so-called '*Juncker package*'—named after the current EU president Jean-Claude Juncker—aims at

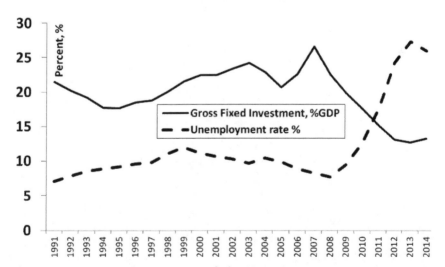

Figure 5.4 Gross Fixed Investment and the Unemployment Rate. *Source*: Ameco Eurostat. Investment as percent of GDP.

mobilizing private as well as public funds through the European Investment Bank to the tune of €300 billion in order to finance investment projects in the EU. The initiative could not have been timelier for Greece and other debt-stricken economies. Greece should participate in the opportunities that lay ahead by organizing a coherent investment plan. In combination with existing structural funds, the new initiative can provide further funding and strategic support in enhancing competitiveness and promoting the export capacity of, and job creation in, the Greek economy.

***

In summary, thanks to the deep recession, Greek debt continued to rise explosively even after an ill-targeted reduction was applied in 2012. One of the most aggravated problems due to the crisis has been the devastation of investment activity and the associated rise in unemployment. There is no doubt that a return to full employment cannot be achieved without a full-fledged recovery of investment activity, and the question is how this could best be encouraged. A change of currency is hailed by many as the most accessible way forward, but the argument is illusory as will be explained in the next part of the book.

NOTES

1. Its level is recorded by Eurostat in the homonymous series of statistical data.

2. The 'snowball' effect is measured by the formula $b(t-1)*(r-g)/(1+g)$, where b is the previous period debt to GDP ratio, r the real interest rate and g the rate of real GDP growth. The effect is increasing with (r) and decreasing with the growth rate. For $r=4\%$, $g=-6\%$ and $b=160\%$, the effect is 17% of GDP per year.

3. A detailed report can be found in Bank of Greece (2014, p. 107).

4. That was on top of the contraction by another -8% during 2008–2010 as a result of the global crisis.

5. At the same time, Portugal's stock decreased by −3%, while Ireland's rose by 5%. Data are from Ameco; series OKND.

6. In economics, this phenomenon is called 'consumption smoothing' and is explained on the basis of the prudent behaviour of households. In Greece, private consumer spending accounted for approximately 70% of GDP throughout the entire period under review. In 2007, prior to the outbreak of the crisis, it stood at 69.60%, while in 2011, the year of the great income reductions, it rose to 74.60% of GDP. In 2013, it fell to 72% of GDP, showing a slight tendency of returning to normal levels. (The calculations were made on the basis of consumption and GDP data in current prices, Ameco Database 2013).

7. See Kolev et al. (2013).

Part III

THE ILLUSIONS

Chapter 6

Change Currency?

Illusions and Miscalculations

Against the backdrop of repeated failures in the adjustment programme, an alternative approach started to take root in Greece by supporting the exit from the common currency and the return to national monetary policy—cum a default on debt payments. The Grexit thesis is built upon a variety of heterogeneous arguments, ranging from the structure of the Eurozone as an incomplete Monetary Union to the supposedly idiosyncratic place of Greece in the western world. Two important facts are missed: first that the Eurozone has been greatly improved since the crisis, and, second, nobody in history has deliberately chosen to replace a good and stable currency with an inferior one.

6.1. THE FADING ROLE OF GREECE

6.1.1. Enter Uncertainty

During the tumultuous five-year period, 2010–2015, the possibility of Greece's exit from the Eurozone has come quite a few times to the forefront. On some occasions, it came as a concealed threat by certain countries, in case Greece refused to undergo a deep fiscal adjustment. On others, it came as a warning by pundits and other analysts that if adjustments were not made, the economy would never be able to regain competitiveness and reduce its gaping external deficit, thus Grexit would be unavoidable.

On yet other occasions, it raised its head as the inevitable outcome of Greece's taking unilateral steps that would be impossible to redress later on. This was almost the case with the referendum that was unexpectedly announced in November 2011 on the measures that the government had just had agreed to implement but then backed off. Had it taken place, the outcome would most likely have been a rejection of the Memorandum and Grexit would probably follow by default. The turmoil was put under control only after the then prime minister resigned and a provisional coalition government was formed.[1] The government negotiated the debt reduction and PSI schemes and, in exchange, adopted the second Memorandum.

However, the possibility of a Grexit resurfaced a little later, because of the inconclusive general elections in May 2012, in which the ruling socialist party was decimated and Syriza occupied the second place. In the run up to a second round of elections in June, Syriza was further advancing by pledging a termination of the austerity programme and denouncing the insistence on keeping the euro as a monetary fetish. Uncertainty sparked a massive withdrawal of bank deposits, and new liquidity shortages drove the economy to an even deeper recession. The Grexit fear subsided only after the centre-right party finally won the elections and a coalition government was formed and duly opted for Greece's unwavering stay in the Eurozone. Post-2015 elections, uncertainty rules again, as the negotiations between the left-wing government and the Troika were protracted and pressure for an all-out collision with European institutions was increasing among the rank and file. All these developments not only burdened the economy with new uncertainties and risks, but also affected the perception of the country at large.

6.1.2. From Mainstream to the Margin

Apart from the economic shockwaves that the Greek situation has wrought on the Eurozone's economy, Greece's role in the European process has been seriously undermined, as well as its regional influence, overturning many aspects that, up to that time, were taken for granted. In the previous three decades, Greece had been increasingly included in all European integration processes, reaping major benefits in terms of economic stability, enhanced growth and political influence. It was a permanent recipient of structural programmes that facilitated the drastic upgrade of its infrastructures, participated from day one in the creation and circulation of the euro and played a key role in EU's enlargement in 2003 with the accession of ten new member states.

The entry of Cyprus in the EU, the rapprochement with Turkey at the 1999 Helsinki summit and the implied 'transformation' of bilateral disputes into Europe-wide ones, as well as the strategic decision to side with the Franco–German opposition to the Iraqi war in 2003, promoted Greece to a major regional player. In the Balkans, the realization of large-scale investments by Greek private-sector interests in the local manufacturing and banking sectors reinforced Greece's position and influence, helping the country to overcome the shadows cast by its ill-advised solidarity to the Milosevic regime and the friction with neighbouring FYROM over the latter's name.

This image of Greece has all but vanished today. Public opinion in the Eurozone perceives Greece as a bottomless pit that swallows European taxpayers' money and a perpetually maladjusted partner, as compared to the other crisis countries Ireland and Portugal. These countries have also entered the Support Mechanism, though each one for its own different reasons, but have accomplished the adjustment programme in due course and by avoiding devastating recession. In Eastern Europe, Greece is currently perceived as the ultimate anti-model of economic behaviour, especially after the formation of a Eurosceptic government with some visible pro-Russian leanings. In the neighbouring Balkan countries, the recognition of Greece's role as Europe's representative in the 'neighbourhood' has been replaced by a tacit disentanglement, aimed at avoiding any stain on their own progress towards European integration. Turkey's strong economic growth up to now and its pressured Messianic role in the developments in North Africa and the Middle East simply make Greece's strategic disorganization seem even more worrying.

6.1.3. The Hidden Agenda

Inasmuch as domestic recovery remains fleeting and uncertainty continues to prevail throughout the Eurozone—at least for some time—it is obvious that Greece's financial, social and geopolitical situation will continue to deteriorate, leading to the re-emergence and propagation of Grexit scenarios. It is worth noting, however, that a change of currency triggers a series of income and wealth redistribution mechanisms. It is in no way certain that such a redistribution would benefit the many instead of the few. What is diligently withheld from public debate is that any actual improvement in competitiveness, as a result of switching to a cheaper currency, will be based on the reduction of real wages and last only so long as workers are inhibited from claiming a better pay. Moreover, any changes in business fundamentals will be based on this wage reduction, not on structural improvements or unearthed advantages that will miraculously resurface at the sight of the drachma.

Although the arguments in favour of a Grexit fail to mention those redistribution mechanisms, they eagerly appropriate a number of historical incidents, which supposedly demonstrate the superiority of an independent currency as opposed to participation in a currency union. The 1932 crisis, when the drachma abandoned the Gold Standard, is considered by many to be a godsend that must be repeated today as soon as possible, in order to lead the Greek economy to growth and employment. The 2002 crisis in Argentina, when the local currency's peg to the dollar was abandoned leading to a rapid devaluation, is considered to be a foolproof recipe for economic revival in today's Greece.

6.2. THE EXIT ADVOCATES

Interestingly enough, more and more people have come to view the possibility of Grexit not as a disaster but as a new opportunity for the country, arguing that only a policy based on a new currency and a large devaluation can boost exports and employment. They deliberately ignore the second-stage consequences of the new currency's collapse and, consequently, base their proposal on an overall theory against Greece's membership of the euro. A range of specious—albeit disparate—arguments are presented to support the exit: from economic analyses focused on competitiveness to cultural and political aphorisms that Greece is a 'unique case' and cannot afford (or should not) being a member of a Western European family. These theories can be classified into the following three categories, which are briefly discussed in the following.

6.2.1. A Wholesale Discrediting of the Euro

Some of those who claim that Greece should not have joined the euro in the first place often resort to an outdated and repeatedly disproved argumentation that flourished in the United States during the 1990s, enriched with the Eurosceptic rhetoric and outright opposition to the process of European integration.

As a matter of fact, initially almost all American economists were critical towards the creation of the euro. Some of them were actually betting that the euro would collapse in just ten years, but they lost—at least so far. However, their individual arguments against the euro were too diverse to be taken at face value. The views of liberal American economists (for example, Paul Krugman) were based on the 'growth hypothesis', in other words on the belief that a government must intervene and devalue its currency in order to improve its trade balance. The views of conservative economists (e.g. Milton Friedman) were based on the 'monetarist hypothesis', according to which governments should not tinker with exchange rates at all. Obviously, it is impossible to view both of these arguments as correct, just to give the artificial impression that all leading US economists were unanimously against the euro for some common reason.[2]

As it turned out, the euro took the middle road between the two versions, that is, adjusting its exchange rate in order to deal with international changes in competitiveness, albeit leaving the exchange rate among the countries of the Eurozone unchanged. This was meant to put an end to the mutually hostile and fruitless intra-European devaluations, which had caused many woes during the 1930s after the collapse of the Gold Standard, as well as in the 1990s after the collapse of the Exchange Rate Mechanism.

Most likely the US economists' concerns regarding the way the euro was set up were purely academic. This, however, was definitely not the case for the Anglo-American financial system, which was an ardent opponent of the euro as its introduction would undermine the dollar's international role: the new currency would gradually become a reserve currency for many countries, at least partly displacing the greenback. This is the reason why we still see many analysts being all too ready to rise up against the euro and the Eurozone's authorities, but not against the dollar and the corresponding US institutions, even when the policies of the latter are even more controversial in facing the crisis.

A similar convergence of extreme views against the euro could be also seen in Europe's political scene. The nationalist right—such as Le Pen's Front National in France and the Lega Nord in Italy—considered the euro to be a means of subjugating the nation. The communist parties of the time denounced the euro as a means of subjugating the working class. However, the workers' unions, which possibly knew better than their self-appointed political instructors, were ardently in favour of the new currency, because they knew that it would boost both the European economy and their wages, as was indeed the case at least until the global financial crisis. Even when the 2008 crisis broke out, the euro offered a haven of stability within the global storm. Although the 2010 debt crisis brought about many changes, it did not lead to a monetary collapse, and the scenarios concerning the dismantling of the Eurozone have not—at least yet—been verified.

6.2.2. Idiosyncratic Greece

In the 1990s, the only domestic force to oppose Greece's signing of the Maastricht Treaty was the Greek Communist Party (KKE), as part of its overall opposition to the European Union. However, after the 2010 debt crisis we saw the emergence of many views, which, in hindsight, consider Greece's membership of the Eurozone to be a fundamental mistake. In its place, they propose a different orientation for the country, not only in monetary but also in geopolitical terms. Subscribers to the concept of Greece's geopolitical and cultural uniqueness are implicitly, if not explicitly, echoing the famous theories by Samuel Huntington regarding the 'clash of civilizations'. According to them, Greece is running its own historical course and has its own religious identity, which brings her closer to the Slavic nations and Russia than to Western European societies.[3]

Following the crisis, the theory regarding Greece's detachment from the European process was enriched with a 'destiny theory', according to which the country is doomed to repeat the failures of the past.[4] For example, an American analyst paralleled the Greek economy to a 'permanent basket case', which never managed to rise up to international standards and, inevitably, sooner or later had to abandon the effort.[5] In order to support the prediction that Greece will leave the Economic and Monetary Union, the argument pointed to Greece's departure from the Latin Monetary Union in the nineteenth century. This argument betrays an abysmal ignorance of history. What is really striking in this case is that, although it was still facing chronic problems of poverty and underdevelopment a few decades after its independence in 1821, Greece was able to be part of a strong international union as early as 1868. Admittedly, Greece was forced to leave the union after accumulating unbearable debts in the aftermath of its defeat in the ill-advised Greco-Turkish war of 1897. But even so Greece managed to return to the Latin Union in 1910, thus belying her supposed 'destiny'.

Those in favour of a Grexit often resort to historical precedents that seemingly vindicate the decision to abandon a certain currency and adopt a new one. And as for them, the only remedy now is presumably a new exit that would restore economic growth. The example used to illustrate this case is Greece's recovery after leaving the Gold Exchange Standard, the monetary system that prevailed in the interwar period. Greece's exit in 1932 has in the past few years been presented by the international media in the same context of an inescapable failure. This argument again ignores the fact that, given the requirements of that era, it was a real feat for Greece to manage to become part the system in 1928, despite the staggering economic and social problems it was facing. Moreover, the argument very conveniently suppresses the fact that almost all developed countries of that era also abandoned the same system. Many of them, as a matter of fact, did so before Greece, but no one is tempted to reproach them for perpetual failure. More details of the episode and its consequences are given in chapter 7.

6.2.3. Grexit as the Necessary Response to the Current Crisis

The views of this category are the most interesting, because they refer to currently existing problems of the Greek economy and presume that the exit from the euro is either inevitable, owing to Greece's inability to meet the requirements emanating from its membership, or the imperative option that will enable the economy to recover. According to Nouriel Roubini, an international economist renowned for his doom-like assessments, Greece from the very onset of the crisis should have had defaulted, leaving the euro and reinstating the drachma, which would then be drastically devalued in order to deal with mass unemployment.[6] Others believe that in case Greece leaves the euro, not only will she be able to correct the dwindling competitiveness, but she will also be able to implement a series of market reforms that would restore strong growth rates.[7]

The mechanisms that are set in motion whenever a currency is devalued or replaced by a weaker one are later described in chapter 12, and it is shown that they are likely to work against those whom they are ostensibly to benefit. Prior to this analysis, two relative historical analogies are examined in the following chapters.

6.3. NOBODY CHANGES A GOOD CURRENCY

Undoubtedly, there have been many numismatic changes and currency replacements since ancient times, and most probably there will be more in the future. It is, nonetheless, telling that throughout the economic history of the world there is not a single example of a country that deliberately abandoned its currency because it was strong and reliable. On the contrary, societies were dismayed when their currency lost its value, and wanted to replace it with a stronger and more reliable one. In the fourth century BC, Dionysius of Syracuse adulterated the coin in order to repay the war debt, and following the public outcry tried to replace it with a purer one. In ancient Athens, Aristophanes denounced the degradation of the coin as a typical feature of the city's decline following its defeat in the Peloponnesian war. Echoing public feelings, he longed for the era of 'fair' coinage, which had now been put out of use: [8]

> all the fairest of the fair. . .
> These we use not:
> but the worthless pinchbeck coins. . .

The debasement of the coin was even more pronounced during, and in many aspects precipitated, the decline of the Roman Empire. Roman emperors kept on issuing new coins as the previous ones lost their value, leading to the complete monetary collapse that occurred during Diocletian's reign. This is why Constantine the Great, after being proclaimed Augustus in the Eastern Roman Empire, introduced the golden *solidus*, which immediately became the dominant means of exchange and reserve currency of the then known world, and remained so for many centuries afterwards.

This gold-based system was followed, among many others, by England as a means for eradicating inflation in the seventeenth century, by Iron Chancellor Bismarck in 1871 for turning Germany into a reliable and unified economy, by the United States in the late nineteenth century to cope with the multitude of different dollars used by each state, and several others.

Even when a country abandons a currency peg and reintroduces a devaluation policy, it does so because its *own* currency is weak and is no longer able to follow the stronger foreign one. But, until now at least, there has been absolutely no case of a country that had its own strong currency and deliberately replaced it with a weaker one.

What is common, however, is that every devaluation and introduction of a weaker currency sets in motion certain income and wealth redistribution mechanisms. Simply put, currency changes have their winners and losers. This is either because some people become richer or poorer in absolute terms than they were before, or because some people become much better off than others, in relative terms, and inequality is thus exacerbated. The recent history of Greece and that of other countries provides a lot of evidence on both effects as examined below.

All cases of voluntary currency change in history occurred because the public had lost confidence in the existing currency and resorted to barter or started adopting foreign coins as means of exchange. The same happens in modern history, as for example:

- Following the Axis Occupation, Greece changed currency three times, because the drachma was rapidly losing its value and all transactions were performed either in British sovereigns or in kind. The drachma managed to gain credibility only after being pegged to the dollar in 1953, when all currency changes virtually ceased.
- Argentina changed currencies four times during the twentieth century, because each time the previous currency had been rendered obsolete by hyperinflation and nobody wanted to use it as legal tender. The same thing happened in Brazil on six occasions, in Turkey in 2005 and in many other countries.
- Some other countries, realizing that they lacked the institutional credibility for sustaining a stable currency, opted against issuing their own and chose instead, using those of other countries. After gaining its independence from former Yugoslavia in 2006, the new state of Montenegro unilaterally introduced euro as legal tender in all economic activities. The newly created state of Kossovo, another Yugoslavia offspring, acted alike in 2008. It would be inexplicably suicidal for Greece to abandon what other—and a lot poorer—nations strive to acquire even by proxy.

6.4. BAD TIMING

When the failures of the austerity programme became too visible even to its staunch supporters, this admission was used by the drachma lobby as a pretext for claiming that Greece's exit from the Eurozone was, supposedly, the inevitable solution. Instead of leading to a revision of the austerity programme and the adoption of a new approach to debt sustainability, the argument was to throw away the baby, not just the bathwater. This paradox becomes even more pronounced if one takes into account that, in the past few years, the Eurozone has taken major steps towards dealing with crises and ensuring the smoother functioning of the currency union. More specifically:

- First the European Financial Stability Facility and then the European Stability Mechanism have been established with the aim of directly providing liquidity to countries facing credit asphyxiation.
- The ECB is now able to perform unlimited open market transactions whenever a country faces severe upward pressures on its borrowing costs. Although the Quantitative Easing had not yet been fully used in practice, its design and first stage of implementation provided a deterrent against speculative plans.
- A new mechanism for the supervision of state budgets was introduced in 2012 and put in operation in 2013 through the Fiscal Compact, in order to prevent large fiscal derailment and the unbridled increase of public debt.[9] It also includes measures that will check the gap between surplus and deficit countries within the Eurozone.
- The Banking Union is in preparation, in order to guarantee the citizens' savings and supervise the operation of banks in order to prevent their involvement in high-risk activities, a frequent phenomenon in many countries that has contributed to the 2008 crisis.
- New mechanisms for the provision of assistance to national economies that are hit by asymmetric shocks are being examined.

Although the new institutional framework is still short of being a comprehensive system for the economic governance of the Eurozone, it represents a major step forward, as compared to the situation that prevailed just a few years ago. Its importance becomes even greater when taking into account that, had it been established before the crisis, the recessionary impact on European countries could have been much milder. For example, budgetary supervision would have averted the fiscal collapse that occurred in Greece during 2008–2009; the Banking Union would have prohibited Irish and Spanish banks from investing in toxic products; and the limits on foreign imbalances would have moderated Germany's surpluses and would have voiced an early warning on the large deficits of the European south.

Even after the crisis, the threat of a mass intervention by the ECB would have staved off the collapse of government bonds, while a central initiative for supporting business activity would have provided a much more efficient response to the crisis than the unilateral efforts of each country. Under such conditions, the continuation of Greece's membership of the single currency becomes more imperative—not more problematic. The aggravated problems the country is currently facing are not due to the single currency, but to the type and intensity of the austerity policies that were implemented. The contradictory result of meeting the deficit targets, while failing to stabilize the debt is the most pronounced evidence of ill-planning and bad implementation.

***

Leaving the euro would prove to be just another miscalculation, on top of the multitude already experienced by the Greek economy. There has been no historical precedent of a country replacing a good currency with a weak one, just in order to face problems that have been generated in other areas of policy. Although there are still many steps required before the Eurozone acts as a full-fledged economic union, it has nevertheless developed a number of mechanisms that will allow it to respond better to future crises. A Grexit would simply miss these new opportunities, and make the country even more isolated—not more attractive—on the world stage. Similar conclusions can be drawn from relevant historical episodes that are examined next.

NOTES

1. PM George Papandreou resigned after being severely reprimanded in the European summit in Cannes, France, in November 2011. Initially he suggested that the new government be headed by the president of Parliament, but finally the ex-deputy ECB governor Lucas Papademos was sworn in to provide credibility and trustworthiness in the negotations.

2. An interesting account of anti-euro voices by US academics is presented by Jonung and Drea (2009). Most of the fears expressed against the creation of EMU proved to be groundless.

3. See the article by Huntington (1993).

4. See the article by Vanatta (2012) in Bloomberg.

5. See the article by Hartwitch (2011).

6. Roubini (2011).

7. See the article by Azariadis (2011).

8. Aristophanes, *The Frogs*. Translation by B.B. Rogers.

9. A brief outline of the provisions of the Fiscal Compact can be found in EC (2012c, Box 10, p. 32).

Chapter 7

History Lessons

The Collapse in Interwar Greece

A historical episode that is frequently used by the proponents of Grexit is the abandonment of the Gold Exchange System in 1932, after which Greece devalued the currency and defaulted on its obligations. The popular assumption goes that the economy rebounded strongly afterwards, so that a similar prospect may be within reach after Grexit. This chapter describes several economic indicators to show that the consequences of the 1932 debacle were a lot more painful than assumed. In fact, it was only the tiny industrial production that benefitted from currency collapse, while the predominant agricultural sector suffered abject poverty.

7.1. THE HOPE IN INTERWAR GREECE

In an effort to provide some historical basis to the argument in favour of Greece having its own independent currency, some analysts try to present the 1932 crisis and the country's abandonment of the Gold Standard during the interwar period as a one-way option, which promptly led to the revival of the Greek economy. Correspondingly, the present-day argument is that a similar revival will occur in the wake of a Grexit. The historical facts, however, are quite different, since the 1932 exit neither was a one-way option nor had any spectacular results for the economy of Greece or the other countries of the periphery. As a matter of fact, in the first years following its departure from the system, unemployment soared, poverty spread to the largest parts of the population, and the country entered a prolonged period of destabilization. The economy showed substantial signs of recovery only after 1936, following the establishment of a right-wing dictatorship and the harsh imposition of a

wage containment mechanism. These aspects are very conveniently over-
looked by those in favour of a large devaluation today.

7.1.1. Winning and losing

The 1920s were one of the most tumultuous periods in the history of the modern Greek state, severely damaging national pride, stretching social relations
and disrupting the country's integration in the international system. Exactly
one century after the War of Independence from Ottoman Turkey, Greece was
on a path of national renaissance, thinking and acting as a budding European
power after the Treaty of Sevres in 1920 had awarded Greece with new areas
in the north including Eastern Thrace. It was the country 'lying on two conti-
nents and surrounded by seven seas'. But three years later came the Asia Minor
disaster, with the sacking of Smyrna and the mass ethnic cleansing of Greek
populations by the Young Turks. The Lausanne Treaty of 1923 erased most
of Greece's territorial gains from her participation in the First World War and
the country once again became a tangle of political conflict and social misery.

7.1.2. The Post-1922 Economic Collapse

In turn, political instability led to further economic decline and unstoppable
social outbreaks. The exorbitant military expenditures of the previous years
could no longer be serviced either by internal borrowing or by resorting to
foreign lenders. The cost of borrowing shot up above 26%, four times higher
than wartime interest rates. Domestic capital fled to London banks, while
foreign markets shied away from a defeated and insolvent state. Public debt
reached 100% of GDP—a very high level for that period—while interest and
principal payments became a noose around the Greek economy. In 1927, they
exceeded 10% of GDP, soaking up an increasing portion of tax revenues,
which also plummeted because of the overall chaos.

The state was totally unable to find the resources required for restoring the
economy, and *nolens volens* resorted to the only available option: it printed
copious quantities of money, leading to the total depreciation of the drachma.
In 1923, the value of the drachma against the British pound and the US dollar
was reduced sixteenfold as compared to the exchange rates prevailing at the end
of the First World War.[1] Since most of the debt was owed abroad, its servicing
became even more unbearable after the rapid devaluation of the drachma.

Soon, the economy was ensnared in high inflation and massive unemployment. In the two years of the 1922–1923 debacles, inflation rose to 150%.
As a result of the high inflation, the purchasing power of real wages evapo-
rated, and the poorer social strata were driven into despair. The ranks of the
unemployed were further augmented by the arrival of refugees, as well as

demobilized soldiers from the Asia Minor front,[2] creating an explosive situation in the labour market. As a result of the riots that ensued, the General Confederation of Labour was outlawed in 1923, albeit this did not put an end to social unrest, which became even more acrimonious.

The extensive fragmentation of arable land, due to repeated allotment policies, played a decisive role in keeping agricultural production and farming income at persistently low levels. Neither did manufacturing manage to pick up the benefit of successive devaluations, since production was constrained by the inadequacy of domestic demand, while businesses could not grow and stand up to international competition due to lack of investment capital.

7.1.3. Reintegration in the International System

This created an urgent need for the wholesale restructuring of the economy, as well as for dealing with the country's aggravated social problems before they led to a total collapse. Both tasks required new resources, either for financing development projects or for establishing tolerable living conditions for the refugees. Naturally, top priority was given to the country's reintegration in the international system, with the aim of restoring domestic stability and attracting the requisite foreign capital.

The dominant international system of that time was the Gold Exchange Standard. It was re-instated by the Genoa Conference in 1922 to replace the pre-war Gold Standard and came into force the following year, when a wave of hyperinflation swept Germany, threatening to contaminate other economies. Soon, the Gold Exchange Standard became the self-evident stabilization option and the indispensable mechanism for seeking funds in international markets.

Greece's economy was too weak to rush in, but Britain's entry in 1925 increased the urgency for two reasons: First, because the majority of its creditors were based in the City of London and would, therefore, view Greece's participation as a 'seal of approval' and a guarantee for the repayment of their loans.[3] Second, because an economic alignment with Britain could also create the conditions for a strategic rapprochement with the main powers. This would facilitate the restoration of Greece's role in the geopolitical scene, which had so ingloriously been ended by the defeat in Asia Minor.

7.2. RISE AND FALL, AGAIN

7.2.1. The Entry to the Gold Exchange

Soon after the 1928 elections, the Bank of Greece was established as the new financial regulator; Greece and Britain agreed on a BPS 4 million reconstruction loan; and in May 1928 Greece joined the Gold Exchange Standard at a rate of 375 drachmas per BPS, which became the reference currency. This *de facto* implied an exchange rate of 77 drachmas per US dollar, as well as fixed exchange rates with the other currencies that participated in the system.[4]

Inflation immediately fell below 5%, exports rose and the chronic trade deficit showed some improvement. The purchasing power of wages was stabilized, and this, in turn, boosted domestic demand. Output increased, the economy came out of a prolonged recession and employment picked up. The government capitalized on this favourable environment to promote a series of remarkable economic reforms. It established the Agricultural Bank to facilitate the extension of credit to small farmers, and the Mortgage Bank to provide manufacturers with land in an orderly fashion. Taxation was restructured and revenues rose by 6% of GDP. However, as a result of the continuous increase in expenditures, this led to a minor and only temporary improvement of public deficits.

The system was shocked by the 1929 Crash in the United States, which soon trapped the entire global economy in a recession. Greece had not yet been fully integrated in the international system, and thus avoided the first wave of the crisis; however, she had also not yet fully implemented the necessary structural reforms and, as a result, it was still seen as vulnerable by the increasingly restless international markets.

The lack of coordination among the countries in the GES exacerbated the impact of the crisis and soon each country started pursuing beggarthy-neighbour policies. During the 1930s, the richer and more developed countries over-accumulated foreign exchange reserves in order to protect their own currencies, thus reducing global liquidity and leading the countries of the periphery to credit asphyxiation.[5] This undermined every effort to reach a consensus regarding a coordinated exit from the crisis and soon forced one country after the other to abandon the Gold Standard.

7.2.2. Futile Defence and Exit

In an effort to cope with the lack of borrowing, Greece adopted strict austerity measures that deepened recession, while the decrease in international demand left no room for an export-led growth. The country's foreign exchange reserves started falling after 1930 as a result of growing fears over a potential devaluation of the drachma, and were only temporarily stabilized when the government announced an even stricter budget for the fiscal year 1931–1932.

On the international level, Greece had placed all its hopes on aligning with Britain, not only because of its dependence on London-based lenders, but also because the head of the League of Nations' Financial Committee was a director with the Bank of England. In order to demonstrate its alignment with

Britain's economic policy choices, in the summer of 1931 the Bank of Greece went forward with an impressive—and unfortunately fatal—act of solidarity: it converted a large part of its foreign currency reserves to pounds sterling, in order to assist the Bank of England in its own struggle to stave off severe devaluation pressures.[6]

Despite this unprecedented support to her ally, things soon took the worst possible turn for Greece. In September 1931, Britain unilaterally decided to abandon the Gold Exchange Standard and devalued the pound sterling by 25% against the dollar. The Greek government was thunderstruck. Not only because it had not been asked by Britain to follow suit, but also because the value of its foreign exchange reserves automatically shrank, thus further weakening Greece's sole—and solitary—defence against speculative pressures.

Although she had obviously been left behind the events, Greece ignored the oncoming speculative wave and did not join Britain in leaving the system. With profuse recklessness, she chose to maintain the drachma's peg to the dollar at the previous rate, as if nothing had happened. Foreign exchange reserves started to plummet and within six days were reduced to half. The three emergency laws that were passed in September and October 1931 and in February 1932, imposing capital controls, proved to be nothing more but part of a panic-driven death spiral: some measures are taken, control is soon lost, and new measures are taken, until the final collapse. With reserves exhausted, the country finally yielded in April 1932 and abandoned the Gold Exchange Standard. The drachma was immediately devalued by 85% against the dollar, only to be further devalued later. At the same time, the government unilaterally defaulted on its debts, automatically causing borrowing costs to skyrocket and the country was completely shut out of international markets. And this is when a new tragic period began.

7.3. THE AFTERMATH OF DEFAULT

After the default, many people believed that the government had at last been relieved from its unbearable obligations towards its lenders, also expecting that the devaluation of the drachma would automatically restore the growth momentum of the Greek economy. In practice, though, the economy faced even more adverse conditions.

7.3.1. Domestic Recession

Soon after the devaluation, inflation started rising again leading to the immediate reduction of real wages. Although this made production more competitive, it simultaneously caused domestic demand to shrink, and eventually became the decisive factor, for a series of reasons:

The value of agricultural production, which at that time accounted for 50% of total economic activity, suffered a severe drop: on the one hand, because prices plummeted as a result of the devaluation and, on the other hand, because international demand decreased as other countries entered recession. Industrial output increased significantly, but still was not enough to affect the overall activity, as manufacturing accounted for a mere 9% of national output.[7] As a result, total economic activity fell below pre-crisis levels, and was restored only three years later. During this transition, unemployment continued to rise, as firms were sceptical of a definitive improvement in the economic climate and ceased hiring. Others were forced to shut down, because they were unable to meet the increased loan amortization payments.

Barry Eichengreen, a renowned expert on that period, describes the panic that prevailed when, one after the other, Central Banks rushed to convert their foreign currency reserves to gold, thus dramatically reducing international liquidity and causing the weakest countries to asphyxiate. According to Eichengreen:[8]

> The resulting vacuum was disastrous. The chaotic liquidation of foreign exchange reserves made credit scarce and put upward pressure on interest rates at the worst possible time, making it hard for firms to finance not only international transactions but domestic investment, as well. Disorderly exchange-rate movements disrupted trade flows, making it harder for countries to export their way out of the Depression. Nations now losing gold and foreign exchange reserves imposed capital controls that hindered foreign investment. *It took years, well into the post-war period, for international trade and investment to recover to the levels that had prevailed prior to the collapse* of the international monetary system. (Emphasis added).

Such effects were even more pronounced in weaker economies and Greece in particular, for which access to international credit became a lot more stringent.

7.3.2. Inability to Borrow

The country's foreign exchange reserves remained in a dire state and only in 1934 were they, more or less, stabilized at the level they were at the beginning of 1931, when the pressure had begun. So, the drachma continued to fall, fuelling inflation and reducing purchasing power. Following the default, the state was relieved from having to make interest payments and principal loan repayments, but the large drop in incomes dragged down government revenues, and the fiscal situation showed no marked improvement.

Combined with the default, this caused financing costs to skyrocket. The cost of issuing Greek government bonds, from around 6% before the collapse, increased more than sixfold. It took several years for it to fall to 25%, just around the level in the wake of the Asia Minor disaster.

The quintessence of a nation's creditworthiness is the ability to borrow from foreign markets in its own currency. By defaulting on her external debt, Greece forfeited this option for many decades. It could still get loans, but always under a foreign currency clause, which meant that even the slightest devaluation of the drachma made debt even more unbearable. When it started resorting to domestic debt, however short-term, the cost was very high, as domestic investors wanted to be compensated both for the high inflation, and for the risk of a new default. It took more than six decades, when Greece was firmly on the path of joining the EMU, to regain the creditworthiness that was lost by the failure of 1932. The first foreign loan in drachmas was issued in 1998, in the form of ten-year fixed-rate bonds.

7.4. POLITICAL COLLAPSE

Economic hardship caused acute social unrest and led to uncontrollable political developments; this, of course, would not have happened, had the abandonment of the Gold Standard provided Greece with the growth advantage that many expected then and Grexit followers proclaim today.

In contrast, the country soon entered a prolonged period of instability, strongly resembling the period that followed the Asia Minor disaster: in the four years after the collapse there were four elections (1932, 1933, 1935 and 1936), one major party abstention from voting, one attempt to assassinate the former prime minister and four coups d'état. Two of those coups were attempts to restore the Liberal Party in power, and—after failing—their leaders faced the firing squad. The third coup was royalist and led to the restoration of the monarchy through a rigged referendum. The fourth coup, in August 1936, adjourned the parliament indefinitely and imposed a right-wing dictatorship.

The authoritarian regime immediately put a complete ban on industrial action, thousands of trade unionists were put in prison or sent to exile, pay-raise demands ceased and all parties of the Left were outlawed. This is how the wage containment mechanism that was described in chapter 6 was set up, and this is how more favourable conditions for production were established. Manufacturing activity was substantially increased both through the use of protectionist measures and defence procurement, as the drums of war sounded louder throughout Europe.

However, the above was still not enough to alleviate high unemployment. To achieve this goal, the regime formed the Labour Battalions, a semi-military formation where jobless workers and landless farmers were employed en masse at public works on a minimum wage.

All this may provide a better understanding of the kind of economic 'miracle' that supposedly followed the currency collapse. In some developed countries, economic recovery did occur because their currencies were freed from the '*golden fetters*' of the interwar system.[9] In Greece, economic recovery was made possible thanks to the '*iron fetters*' of the authoritarian regime.

***

In retrospect, the consequences of Greece exiting the Gold Exchange Standard in 1932 were dramatic, both in economic and political terms. Though participation had become untenable after the British exit in 1931, Greece was in no position to reap any serious benefits from the massive devaluation that followed and the ensuing decrease in real wages. Social protests erupted to such a degree that the political instability led to the imposition of an autocratic regime a few years later. Another example that is enthusiastically offered as a possible alternative to the current malaise in Greece is Argentina's collapse and default in 2002. In fact, some of the shortcomings of the 1932 debacle are found to be common and equally problematic with the modern version.

NOTES

1. To be precise, the drachma lost 1612% of its value against the pound sterling and 1686% against the US dollar. Source: Bank of Greece.

2. Almost one million Greeks from Asia Minor fled to Greece as refugees. Moreover, in accordance with the population exchange convention, large numbers of Muslims left Northern Greece bound for Turkey, while a smaller-scale population exchange was also agreed on with Bulgaria.

3. As described in Bordo and Rockoff (1996).

4. The BPS/USD exchange rate was set at 4.86, exactly equal to its value before the First World War. However, the British economy had been greatly weakened as compared to that of the United States, and this exchange rate was severely criticized as non-competitive and non-sustainable. In his book *Essays in Persuasion*, Keynes called this exchange rate a 'relic of pre-war policy' and was highly critical of Churchill, then Britain's chancellor of the exchequer.

5. For an analysis of the asymmetry problem, see Wandschneider (2008).

6. Similar measures were taken by other countries of the British Commonwealth, in order to help the metropolis deal with speculative pressures. But Greece was not a member of the Commonwealth and neither had benefitted in previous years by

the growth of trade between these countries, nor was to enjoy any kind of economic favour from Britain in the years to come.

7. For more details, see Christodoulaki Olga (2001), Kopsidis (2012), as well as Psalidopoulos (2011) and Costis (1986).

8. Eichengreen, B. (2012).

9. As described in the classic essay by Eichengreen and Sachs (1985), The phrase 'Golden fetters' is attributed to Keynes and is widely used to denote the restrictions imposed by membership in an international system of economic rules.

Chapter 8

Modern Lessons

Default and Collapse in Argentina

A more recent example of economic collapse is Argentina after its default in 2002. This chapter describes how wages suffered a prolonged decline in terms of international purchasing power, while inflation once more became endemic. The capital inflows triggered by the devaluation were in fact nothing more than the return of expatriated funds, which led to a drastic redistribution of wealth and income away from the wage-earners.

8.1. DEFAULT AND COLLAPSE

When the Greek debt crisis broke out, many international analysts paralleled the case of Greece with that of Argentina in the early 2000s and suggested that the former should immediately leave the euro in order to avoid a costly battle she could not possibly win.[1] The similarities between the two countries were highlighted in a *New York Times* op-ed, calling Greece to exit the euro and thrive like Argentina did after the collapse.[2] These views were soon endorsed by Paul Krugman and other international economists. Such suggestions were based on two assumptions: first that the Greek economy's problems were reminiscent of the situation in Argentina prior to the collapse and, second, that following the default in 2002, the latter's economy was restored to growth and uninterrupted prosperity.[3] In reality, neither is true. As is shown below, Greece's case is much different and more complex than that of Argentina. The myth of the economic 'miracle' that supposedly followed the default is, anyway, too frail to be used as a guiding example.

8.1.1. Similarities and Differences

Argentina's situation was similar in that it combined increasing indebtedness with a prolonged recession: In 2001, Argentina found itself with an external deficit of 5% of GDP, while its debt burden had almost doubled within a decade, rising to 65% of GDP from 35% in 1990. In 2001, the growth rate was zero and social discontent on the rise. Drastic expenditure cuts made in order to reduce government borrowing, exacerbated recession to such dramatic levels that everyone expected another social upheaval, like the ones that had shaken Latin America in previous decades. Some people saw many similarities with the climate of conflict and unrest that has prevailed in Greece in recent years.

However, the differences between the two economies are even more striking, the first and foremost being the exchange rate regime. Argentina had introduced full convertibility with the dollar, albeit the peso continued to exist as the national currency. This way, the currency peg had succeeded in harnessing inflation, but at the cost of high domestic interest rates, which eventually depleted the banks' liquidity and stifled productive investment. Competitiveness was dealt an even harder blow when the neighbouring countries—chiefly Brazil and Chile—devalued their own currencies in order to boost their exports to the United States. Argentina had already locked its exchange rate and this gave rise to the first wave of fear that devaluation was imminent.

In order to appease bearish expectations, the government further increased interest rates, causing borrowing costs to swell. But debt refinancing through domestic sources remained unfeasible, as private capital preferred to exploit the full convertibility regime to the dollar and flee the country. Thus, Argentina found itself excessively dependent on foreign banks, which initially had no qualms about generously extending new loans. The real problem occurred when the successive crises of 1997–1998 in Southeast Asia and Russia caused international interest rates to rise, forcing once again Argentina to set its own increasingly higher in order to maintain the exchange rate. The country soon was exhausted by the high interest payments and resorted to the lending facilities of the IMF. The Fund responded to the call, albeit by imposing harsh fiscal austerity measures that made the recession even deeper.

Thus, the method selected for dealing with the downward pressures on the currency exacerbated their cause, that is, the prolonged recession. The markets immediately discounted the possibility that the government would, sooner or later, be forced to abandon the dollar peg and this made it even harder to obtain fresh financing from the IMF. In each round, the Fund demanded new austerity measures as a guarantee for the repayment of the loans. The spiral became so asphyxiating that it took just two years for the peso to collapse. Immediately after that the social outburst the government thought it would avert by abandoning the exchange rate regime broke out, while the debt spiked even more. To deal with this impasse, Argentina unilaterally defaulted on its debts.

In Greece, there is no similarity with the Argentinean exchange rate regime of that time, simply because by entering the Eurozone the country physically abolished its own national currency. So, given that there is no convertibility, the country does not need to pursue a high interest rate policy in order to maintain the exchange rate. In fact, its case is exactly the opposite to that of Argentina: Greece's Eurozone membership gives it access to cheap money, as a result of the quantitative easing policy implemented by the European Central Bank in the wake of the 2008 crisis.

Second, even if the external deficit becomes excessive there is no fear of a concerted speculative attack against the euro, since any defensive measure will be taken by the Eurozone, which has placed massive reserves at the disposal of the ECB. Besides, the Eurozone as a whole usually shows a balanced, and sometimes surplus, current account. What happened in 2001 in Argentina, in 1997 in Malaysia and Thailand or in 1992 in the United Kingdom during the ERM crisis, is not applicable in the case of Greece. This is a major defensive advantage offered by euro membership, which ensures that the country's currency cannot be targeted by speculators. On the other hand, though, it does not cure any of the problems caused by high indebtedness, external deficits and, above all, deep recession.

8.1.2. The Convenient Myths

After the default, Argentina went through a period of social unrest and setbacks. At a certain point, the economy started growing again and, until 2013, the country seemed to have significantly increased its output, eliminated external deficits and healed many chronic social inequality problems. However, a series of events that occurred in the second half of 2013 tarnished this image and many people started to demonize speculators for putting the country once again in their sights. This, however, was not a sudden change of the situation, but the inescapable outcome of the very mechanism used for achieving Argentina's temporary macroeconomic recovery. Therefore, the real extent and sustainability of the Argentinean economic 'miracle' needs to be reassessed.

To begin with the currency facts, in early 2002, the authorities announced that, in order to regain competitiveness, the peso was un-pegged and devalued by 40% against the US dollar. However, as a result of the consequent uncertainty the peso lost 385% of its value in the following six months, nearly ten times more than originally planned. Wage-earners, pensioners, people who lived on social benefits and property owners who collected rents in local currency saw their real incomes fall by three-quarters in just a few months, reliving the nightmare of past Latin American crises. The exchange rate of the Argentinean peso (ARS) was not even stabilized at those levels, because inflation soared and Argentina was under continuous pressure to pursue a further devaluation policy. As a result, the official exchange rate in 2013 closed at almost ARS 7 per USD, and fell even further to ARS 8 per USD in 2014. In practice, this meant that an amount of pesos that in 2000 purchased one hundred foreign goods could barely purchase twelve such items in 2014.

In other respects, the collapse was not so negative. As is usually the case in many such disasters, the collapse of the peso gave rise to a redistribution mechanism that helped the overall economic activity to recover: flight capital was repatriated *en masse*, and its domestic value was now much higher as compared to what it had when fled the country. As a result, in 2012 it soared to 21% of GDP, from 12% in the previous years. Gradually investment followed suit, boosting the real economy. Growth had slumped to −11% in the year of the crisis, but subsequently recovered and stood at almost 10% for a period of five years, to be halted again by the international crisis of 2008. Exports increased, but imports fell even further, owing to the rapid loss of purchasing power. As a result, the external deficit was reversed and, from an average deficit of −2.5% of GDP during the fix currency period 1990–2001 there was an average annual surplus of +2.5% of GDP per year during 2002–2013.

One might be forgiven for thinking that all these developments attest to an economic success, and are rightfully praised by those who recommend it as the perfect solution to Greece's problem. Well, not really, and not for some trivial reason.

8.2. THE HARD FACTS: GROWTH AND WAGES

First of all, the dramatic devaluation obviously increased the competitiveness of Argentina's products worldwide but at the price of dragging the purchasing power of wages to the bottom, which also explains why imports shrank. At the same time, recovery was marred by default-induced distortions, and therefore it was neither impressive as compared to the recovery of other economies in the region, nor resilient enough to withstand the international pressures exerted after 2008. Long before the international crisis, various analysts were pointing that the recovery went hand in hand with an impoverished population. The rekindling of the economy in 2003 was interpreted not as an achievement of the policies pursued by the government, but as a reflex response caused by the chaos the country was in during the previous year. Paul Blustein describes the situation as follows:[4]

Per capita GDP in 2004, adjusted for inflation, was still about 13 percent below the 1998 level; the shortfall in dollar terms was about 55 percent. Nearly one-fifth of the Argentine labour force was still unemployed ... and about 45 percent of the population was living below the poverty line. The economy was growing mainly by using the massive amounts of spare capacity that had been idled during the steep downturn, with another major source of stimulus coming from sky-high world prices for soybeans and grains.

8.2.1. Real wages

More is revealed by a systematic look at developments regarding inflation and the average real wage during the twenty-year span 1992–2012, so as to cover both the periods before and after the collapse. If the real wage is calculated by using the official data on the basis of constant 2012 pesos, one can see from Figure 8.1 that it remained practically unchanged during the entire period of exchange rate stability, which was until the year 2001. After the crisis, it fell by −22% and remained at that level for a few years, before starting to exhibit a strong recovery. In 2012, the real wage appears to have doubled in comparison to its pre-crisis level; and it is precisely this that has led many analysts to contend that there has been a substantial improvement in the income inequality indicators of the country.

The snag, however, is that these calculations are based on the official inflation rate. For quite a few years now, it is believed to be artificially kept much

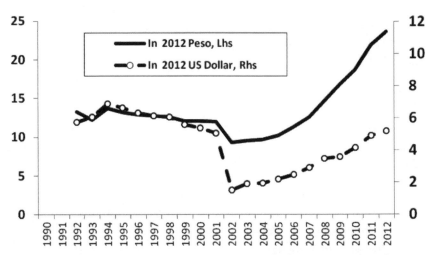

Figure 8.1 Hourly Wage Rates in Argentina, in Purchasing Power Terms. Alternative evaluations based on constant 2012 peso or 2012 US dollar. Valuation is roughly the same over 1992–2001 due to the currency parity. *Source*: http://sedlac.econo.unlp. edu.ar/eng/statistics-detalle.php?idE=38. CPI index from IMF WEO Database. Own calculations.

lower than the actual figure. In 2011, ten years after the collapse, the British daily *Guardian* reported the following about the uncontrollable wave of inflation that is hitting Argentina's economy:[5]

> Inflation is the big issue right now. The government says the annual rate is currently just under 10%, but unofficial figures put it as high as 25%. Independent inflation specialists have been heavily fined for not toeing the government line and it's even alleged the state had words with McDonald's so they wouldn't be embarrassed in the Economist's Big Mac index.[6] Economists argue that, *taking this inflation into account, the country's growth could be pushed down into negative figures.* (Emphasis added).

This is why an objective comparison can only be made if the real wage is calculated in dollar terms, thus revealing its purchasing power in international terms. The picture that emerges with the use of this method is similar to the calculation previously obtained for the decade 1992–2001 as a result of the then prevailing fixed exchange rate parity. But it is radically different in regard to the next decade. In 2002, real wages fell by −70%, reflecting the rapid devaluation of the peso and, despite their gradual recovery, in 2012 still remained −14% below the average during the stabilization period.

A comment is due here about Greece. For comparison purposes, consider that the Memorandum led to a wage reduction of −23%, much more moderate than the income collapse that took place in Argentina in 2002–2012. Given that the internal devaluation sparked such strong protest from trade unions, it is difficult for anyone to argue that the answer to the current recession lies in a regime that will cause an even worse, and much more prolonged, deterioration of real wages.

8.2.2. Inequalities

When a disaster strikes, its consequences are asymmetrical, and the inequality between the rich and poor becomes worse. The drop in purchasing power did not hit all social classes the same. As is usually the case with economic upheavals, low-income earners are less likely to succeed in defending their purchasing power, while the better-off safeguard themselves against risks by dispersing their portfolios in different currencies and investments. This is exactly what happened in interwar Greece and modern Argentina.

The course of inequalities following the devaluation has been the subject of many analyses. A recent research report by the World Bank presents a systematic study of developments in income inequalities in Argentina: The facts presented in the study show that the well-known Gini coefficient of inequality[7] increased from 0.50 in 2000 to 0.54 in 2002, and subsequently fell to 0.44

in 2010 owing to the growth of employment.[8] On the basis of these facts, the report concludes that inequality was reduced *after* the crisis. But this is just an artefact highly sensitive to the definition of the sample. The specific result was obtained simply as the authors conveniently included the collapse year 2002 in the period of exchange rate stability—a clearly arbitrary choice. If 2002 is included—as is the reasonable thing to do—in the post-peg devaluation period, then, the picture changes completely. According to the same data, the average inequality for the period 2002–2010 is almost the same with that for the period 1992–2001. Obviously, there is absolutely no factual base to celebrate any meaningful reduction in inequality.

To avoid time selection sensitivity, another approach that employs the ratio of the income of the richer 10% to the income of the poorer 10% is adopted in each particular year. The higher the ratio, the greater is the inequality between the very rich and the very poor. As shown in Figure 8.2, the value of the ratio almost doubled in the crisis year of 2002, and remained high for many years.[9] It started to decrease only after 2005, when the government made generous increases in social benefits and transfers in order to fight the spread of poverty. Nonetheless, the effect of these measures is strongly moderated too, when accounting for higher inflation is included. In a more visual way, the mass looting of stores in 2013 brought back images of 2002 and raised the embarrassing question of whether things had actually gotten better for low-income groups.

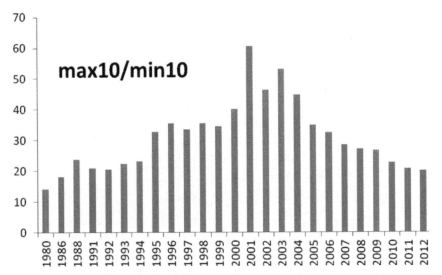

Figure 8.2 Inequality Index in Argentina, by Income Deciles. *Source*: Microdata from household surveys. Socio-Economic Database for Latin America and the Caribbean (CEDLAS and The World Bank) 2014.

Finally, it is worth noting two peculiarities of Argentina's case, which were instrumental to the country's economic recovery as opposed to the case of Greece today: the strong growth of the global economy in the years following the collapse of the peso; and the high exportability of Argentina's products (e.g. coffee, soya beans, meat, etc.) which immediately benefitted from global demand and high international prices. Neither of these two conditions is present in the current case of Greece: first, because both the European and the global economy are still going through a period of slow growth, and, second, because export performance is only marginally affected by changes in wages, as we saw in chapter 4.

Even Argentina did not, however, witness any spectacular recovery when compared with other neighbouring countries. The obvious example is Brazil, whose per capita GDP in the mid-1990s was almost half that of Argentina. Brazil had also adopted a fixed exchange rate policy for its own currency, the *real*, albeit not as rigid, and without providing for free convertibility with the US dollar, as was the case for the peso. Thus, when the Asian crisis broke out in 1997 and Russia collapsed in 1998, Brazil had more elbow room for adjusting the exchange rate of the *real*, and thus managed to enter a path of strong growth. After 2008, its per capita GDP has been higher than that of Argentina, while Brazil's currency has enjoyed remarkable stability during the past decade. The lesson to be learnt is that what really matters in regard to economic growth is not the devaluation, however large, of the currency, but a sustainable balance between monetary rigor and fiscal adjustment. An optimal combination of these can prevent the erosion of competitiveness due to persistent inflation, as well as the weakening of the economy due to the implementation of harsh austerity programmes.

Inequality was also higher regarding the possession of wealth assets as devaluation made capital repatriation appealing. Flight capital was brought back under the new exchange rate and could then acquire a large part of the national wealth at very low prices. This had been precisely the motive behind the great disinvestment during the speculative period. In the aftermath of the collapse, it became the instrument for the unequal acquisition and redistribution of wealth, and this is where Argentina's case starts having scary similarities to that of Greece.

8.3. A SCARY SIMILARITY: GREAT DISINVESTMENT

In Figure 8.3 a comparison is drawn between the drop in the share of investment in Argentina during the twelve years 1992–2003 and the corresponding share in Greece during the decade 2002–2013 that is over the former. The similarity is striking. To explain this, it suffices to point out another equally

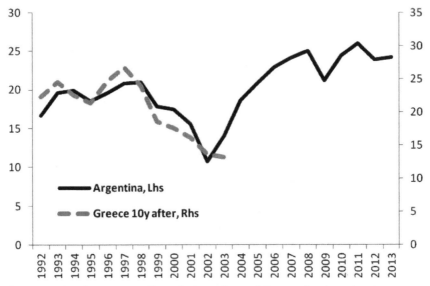

Figure 8.3 **Total Investment Shares in Argentina and Greece.** For Argentina data are per year shown 1992–2013. For Greece per year a decade ahead, i.e. 2002–2013. *Source:* For Greece, Ameco Eurostat. For Argentina, IMF World Economic Outlook Database, April 2014. Original from Ministry of Economy, Argentina.

ominous similarity between Greece and Argentina: the mass outflow of funds from the banking system. In both countries, the rapid drop in investment coincided with a huge reduction of savings and deposits.

In Argentina, the mass capital outflows were triggered by the fear that the devaluation of the peso was imminent. The currency's free convertibility to the US dollar had been established as a means of demonstrating the government's determination to preserve the currency peg. Under this regime, pesos were first converted to US dollars and then fled to foreign bank accounts. In 2001, bank deposits of between USD 80 to 100 billion had fled the country, accounting for almost a third of the country's GDP.

In Greece a convertibility regime is superfluous, thus deposits may simply flee to overseas accounts but can also be just hoarded by people anxious to create a 'nest-egg'. Despite any differences though, similar phenomena of deposit withdrawals were observed in Greece: by the end of 2009, deposits in Greek banks stood at €240 billion, while in 2013 they had fallen to €160 billion. This decrease accounted for almost one-third of GDP, as in the case of Argentina. As shown in Figure 8.4, large outflows began in the first months of 2010 when international markets became increasingly aggressive, but the government of the day could not present a convincing response about how it could manage to deal with the pressures and secure the country's stay in the euro.

Figure 8.4   Bank Deposits in Greek Banks. *Source*: Bank of Greece Conjectural indicators. Table IV.10. Column 5. Deposits and repos of domestic non-MFI with OMFIs, in Greece.

The panic subsided with the signing of the First Memorandum in May 2010 and the consequent provision of financial assistance, but was fanned again whenever uncertainty and scepticism regarding the final outcome of the stabilization effort appeared. The fear of a potential Grexit was revived in autumn 2011, when the idea of holding a referendum fell on the table, as well as during the elections that were held in mid-2012, both cases resulting in mass deposit flight.

Moreover, a series of domestic political initiatives accentuated, instead of minimizing, the incentives for capital flight: the threat of retroactive taxation of bank deposits in 2010, the treatment of bank deposits as proof of undeclared income in 2012 and their use for the automatic payment of tax arrears or other amounts owed to the state in 2013, led many people to withdraw their savings from the system, thus accentuating the wave of disinvestment in the economy. The outflow of deposits from the banking system was partly reversed after the formation of a viable government in June 2012, but remained sensitive to any change in parliamentary majority or in the prospect of political shifts.

Then, when at the end of 2014, Greece entered a new period of electoral uncertainty, withdrawals started to multiply once again. This time, outflows did not cease with elections and the formation of a new government. In fact, they further intensified as negotiations with the European partners on how the programme will continue were protracted and a new wave of Grexit speculation set in. Such uncertainty notwithstanding, the left-wing government targeted bank deposits once more and announced that they would be subject to retroactive tax auditing.

It is quite a mystery why successive Greek governments targeted domestic savings, thus precipitating their flight. It was probably a diversion aimed at drawing attention away from their inability to collect taxes, given that they never showed the same zeal in regard to the identification and taxation of offshore deposits (e.g. the delays in tax auditing the infamous list of undeclared deposits in Swiss banks). Other European governments took a different course of action. For example, the British government's policy was exactly the opposite: a mix of severe pressure and public threats, aimed at exhorting the repatriation of flight capital, which would increase the banks' deposit base and lead to the consequent increase of much-needed investment at a time of crisis.

As long as there is uncertainty regarding the safety of deposits in Greece, either due to the fear of a Grexit or for tax-related reasons, capital flight will persist, exacerbating disinvestment in the real economy and multiplying the effort that will be required for its recovery.

***

The preceding analysis has made clear that Greece is a structurally different case than Argentina was prior to the collapse of 2002. Moreover, the massive devaluation conferred noticeably fewer benefits to Argentina than claimed by the drachma supporters, while the debt default alienated the country from world markets. Much of the investment recovery that took place in Argentina was due to the repatriation of speculative flight capital, thus causing further inequalities and redistribution. To avoid a similar process in Greece, a new strategy should be devised that puts the economy on a path to growth and retains the common currency.

NOTES

1. Among many, see the following: Levy M. and P. Kretzmer, 2012. 'Greece's predicament: Lessons from Argentina'. 16 May. http://www.voxeu.org/article/greece-s-predicament-lessons-argentina; and also *The Economist*, 2012. 'What Argentina tells us about Greece'. 16 Feb. http://www.economist.com/blogs/freeexchange/2012/02/greece-and-euro.

2. See Weisbrot (2011).

3. Krugman, however, seems to have somehow mitigated his position: when speaking in Athens in April 2015, he warned that a Grexit would have dire consequences for the country and the Eurozone; see www.tovima.gr/finance/article/, 18/04/2015.

4. Blustein (2005). The phenomenon is described by the macabre term 'dead-cat bounce', because even the body of a dead cat will bounce if thrown from a great height (pp. 204–205).

5. Baker V. (2011). 'Ten years after economic collapse, Argentina is still in recovery', *The Guardian*, 14/12/2011.

6. In order to estimate inflation rates in various countries, *The Economist*, instead of complex comparisons with the 'housewife's basket', simply publishes the changes in the prices of the flagship item of the MacDonald's fast-food chain. The argument is that the Big Mac is an item that is identical in all countries, and its production encompasses representative goods and services, from agricultural commodities and energy to wages and rents.

7. The Gini coefficient measures income dispersion among different income groups and ranges from 0 (when everybody has the same income) to 1 (when one group has all the income). An increase in its value indicates an increase in inequality.

8. Data are from Lustig, Lopez-Calva και Ortiz-Juarez, (2012), 'Declining Inequality in Latin America in the 2000s: The Cases of Argentina, Brazil, and Mexico'.

9. For more details, see Lusting et al. op.cit. The data are included in Figure 14, p. 20.

Part IV

THE ESCAPE

Chapter 9

Getting It Right

End Recession and Stabilize Public Debt

An alternative policy framework that could be more effective in promoting growth and harnessing indebtedness is presented in this chapter. This alternative programme assumes moderate fiscal targets, a realistic privatization plan and a reallocation of public funds towards more public investments on infrastructure. These measures will instill more growth and reduce debt burden more successfully than endless and excessive austerity. This chapter also assesses how much new capital formation is required for the economy to return to normal. Attractive investment areas and new privatization tools are discussed.

9.1. DEBT SUSTAINABILITY

If the Greek economy remains caught in deep recession, the public debt will never show any actual improvement, no matter how many wage cuts are decided, or how many new taxes are imposed. The Memorandum's failure to stabilize public debt and help the economy recover is now acknowledged even by those who devised it and, for four years, insisted on its rigorous implementation. For example, the IMF report that was published in 2013 contained extensive self-criticism, as well as the warning that the Greek debt remains unsustainable. So, serious action has to be taken soon to reduce the debt burden—and there is good and bad news in regard to that.

The good news is that a large part of Greek public debt now consists of loans extended by other states, instead of private investors and banks. This means that no country would ever launch a speculative attack against Greece in the open market, as had been done in the past by some private lenders. This gives Greece time to put her house in order and eventually stabilize debt. The easier—and for that matter popular—option is to unilaterally default on debt in the hope that the consequences of a fiscal adjustment are circumvented. The bad news, though, is that a "haircut" cannot be anymore imposed mainly on the banks, everybody's convenient scapegoat till recently; instead, it will be presented as a dirty trick against the taxpayers of other countries, causing a severe backlash from their own public. The European states will definitely call for sanctions against Greece, and these could be harsher than the current programme since they will not be accountable to any bank shareholders, but to their own taxpayers.

This is why the only way to find a permanent solution to the Greek debt issue is to give top priority to ending recession and thus avoiding the snowball effect. Further easing could be obtained by extending maturities, reducing servicing costs or consensually cancelling part of it. The no-default framework should go hand in hand with the necessary fiscal adjustments, which should, nonetheless, be much milder than the targets adopted by the existing sustainability scenarios. Otherwise they will, once again, prove to be politically and socially unfeasible. The combination of the appropriate economic growth and fiscal adjustment rates is an issue that has to date led to failures and repeated strategy changes.

For example, when the PSI scheme was implemented in 2012, the European Commission had presented a scenario in which the arrangement would rebase Greek debt and then it could be gradually reduced to 120% of GDP by 2020. Still, this was admittedly a high level, albeit acceptable when taking into consideration the overall situation in the Eurozone. This scenario provided the political rationale for the PSI scheme and was adopted as the official version of the plan for the Greek economy. Unfortunately, it was based on a series of assumptions that are summarized in Table 9.1 and pretty soon proved to be totally unrealistic. The main ones were the following:

Assumption 1: Accelerated Fiscal Adjustment

The Greek economy was expected to show primary deficits equal to 4.50% of GDP after 2013 and for every year thereafter, until 2020. This target was politically and socially unfeasible, at least if the historical record is taken

Table 9.1   Debt Projections by the European Commission, 2012

	2012	2013	2014	2016	2017	2018	2019	2020
Growth rate (%)	−4.70	0.00	2.50	3.00	2.80	2.60	2.50	2.30
Debt %GDP	160	164	161	145	137	130	123	116
Primary surplus %GDP	−1.00	1.80	4.50	4.50	4.50	4.30	4.30	4.30

Source: European Economy, 2012, The Second Adjustment Programme for Greece: Fifth review, Occasional Papers 94, March. Year 2015 not completed.

into account. Even during the convergence process for EMU, when expenses had been substantially reduced and special tax revenues were introduced in order to meet the deficit target, the primary surplus barely exceeded 3% of GDP. With the economy having undergone such a deep recession, with society having been driven to despair and with the mainstream political system in tatters, the target of a primary surplus of 4.50% of GDP was totally unfeasible.

Assumption 2: Fast Resumption of Growth

The same official scenario assumed that the Greek economy would exit recession in 2013 by showing a 1.50% growth rate, and would soon reach annual growth rates of 3.50% up to 2020. The question of how harsh fiscal measures, that were required to achieve such high primary surpluses, could go hand in hand with high growth rates was not easy to answer. Eventually, the European Commission proved once again to be wrong in its forecasts, as the economy actually shrank by −3.8% in 2013.

Had the initial assumptions been valid, post-PSI public debt would have been further reduced to 160% of GDP in 2013 and then would have continued an uninterrupted downward trend towards the 120% target. Neither happened though, and instead the debt increased, approaching pre-PSI levels. The abysmal failure of the EU's assumptions was something new but its cause was not. Once again, by ignoring the recession's impact on a heavily indebted economy, the rapid growth of debt as a percentage of GDP was precipitated.

Responding to this failure, the European Commission prepared a new scenario, based on the actual developments of 2013 and on slightly modified assumptions for the forthcoming years. These assumptions are summarized in Table 9.2; it is obvious that they are also unrealistic and debt forecasts will prove to be wrong too. This scenario was uncritically adopted by the IMF and currently represents the official sustainability analysis[1] of Greek debt. This time, however, the issue is reversed: whereas in 2012 the aim was to persuade European governments to accept the PSI scheme because

Table 9.2 Revised Debt Projections by the European Commission, 2013

	2011	*2012*	*2013*	*2014*	*2015*	*2016*	*...*	*2020*
Growth rate (%)	−7.1	−6.4	−4.20	0.60	2.90	3.70		3.70
Debt %GDP								124
Primary surplus %GDP	−2.30	−1.30	0.00	1.50	3.0	4.50	...	4.50

Source: European Economy, 2013, The Second Economic Adjustment Programme for Greece: Second Review, Occasional Papers 148, May.

this was the only way to put the debt under control, now the aim is to show that the debt is under control so that any talk about a possible new 'haircut' is pointless.

These forecasts were severely challenged by the OECD which, in a recent study, argued that neither large primary surpluses will be achieved, nor can growth feasibly exceed 2% per year under these circumstances. As a result, debt will remain at high levels, standing at 157% of GDP as late as 2020.[2] At that level, debt cannot be considered as sustainable, and consequently, there will have to be a new reduction or some other drastic—though unspecified—intervention. The OECD study once again rekindled the possibility that Greece may not be able to harness its debt and new Grexit fears were ignited. So, the time is ripe to seek other approaches for dealing with it.

9.2. AN ALTERNATIVE SUSTAINABILITY SCENARIO

The antithesis between the forecasts of the EU and those of the OECD brings back on the scene the need for a total reappraisal of the debt issue—and the available options are not unlimited. In fact, they are just three:

a. *Unilateral debt default*, which would lead to a head-on collision with the creditor countries and eventually, to an exit from the euro.
b. *Consensual debt write-off*, which would, nonetheless, require a new Memorandum and new adjustment programmes. Under the current political situation, their approval by the Greek Parliament would be dubious, while their outcome would still be uncertain.
c. *Debt restructuring and growth push*. This is the only option that, by ruling out a default, prevents a new crisis in the relations between Greece and its Eurozone partners and, by not requiring a new Memorandum and relentless fiscal austerity, averts a new round of domestic unrest.

This scenario is based on four pillars, which are markedly different from the assumptions used thus far by the overseeing authorities:

Pillar 1: Gradual Fiscal Adjustment

Fiscal surpluses for the period 2015–2020 can be reduced to 2.50% of GDP, a level that is both realistic and consistent with the past performance of the Greek economy. The OECD also considers this level to be feasible and believes that it may later rise slightly even above 3.20% of GDP.

Pillar 2: Reduction of Interest Rates and Rollover

Over the last few years, the average cost of the loans extended to Greece by the creditor countries was around 3%. A reduction of the interest rate may cut this cost to half. This reduction will not impose any kind of loss on the creditor countries as they borrow at low rates. For example, Germany is borrowing at rates below 1.50% on its long-term bonds, and even lower on its short-term securities.[3] Moreover, the reduction of the interest rate is politically feasible because it will not spark any anti-Greek response from the European countries' public opinion.

Pillar 3: Stronger Growth with New Investments

In order to stabilize the debt, an adequate growth target should be set at 3.50% of Greece's GDP for the next few years. This rate is higher than that suggested by the OECD, albeit it is feasible for the following reason: if the primary surplus is reduced by two percentage points of GDP, the growth rate will be boosted by at least two points, through the operation of fiscal multipliers. In chapter 4, it was shown that fiscal multipliers stand around unity and this justifies the growth effect of lower fiscal austerity.

These assumptions provide the basis for laying out an alternative scenario, which is then compared to that of the EU and the OECD. As shown in Figure 9.1, debt is de-escalating much faster than under the official

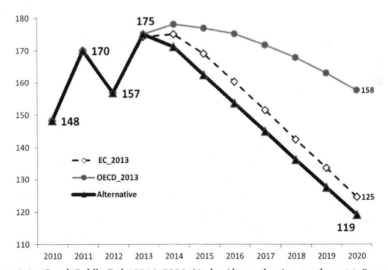

Figure 9.1   Greek Public Debt 2014–2020, Under Alternative Assumptions. (a): European Commission assumptions in 2013. (b):OECD assumptions. (c): Assuming lower public deficits and higher growth. *Source*: For 2010–1013 Ameco Eurostat. Projections from own calculations.

scenarios, despite the fact that the alternative is based on *lower* primary surpluses! It seems paradoxical, but the explanation is simple: when the debt to GDP ratio is high, it is preferable to have stronger growth than greater fiscal adjustment. This is the lesson of the snowball effect that was so recklessly ignored by the austerity programmes, sinking the Greek economy into a severe recession, and making debt even more explosive than it was at its onset.[4]

9.3. A NEW ECONOMIC POLICY

These options, of course, are neither easy to be put in practice nor automatic in delivering the results. Apart from the agreement that has to be reached with the creditor institutions, two further things must be secured: the stability of the fiscal surplus and the realization of the growth target through new investments. The achievement of a primary surplus in 2013 and 2014—though slimmer than initially claimed—makes it possible to set new rules for stabilizing the economy and to take new initiatives for exiting the crisis, as described below.

9.3.1. A New Agreement

The first, and most decisive, step will be to set the country free from the mechanism of the incessant and pointless austerity measures imposed by the Memorandum and put an end to the failed procedure of consultation with the Troika. The aim must be to put an end to the involvement of the IMF, and then form a new agreement between Greece and the European Union.

The current situation in the European Union is conducive to initiatives aimed at changing the stifling austerity regime, as it is increasingly acknowledged that the harsh austerity measures implemented in the past few years were ineffective. The squabble that broke out in 2014 between the IMF and the Eurozone about who failed more can be exploited by Greece for bundling all open issues in a single, strictly European, negotiation framework.

The Memorandum should evolve into an agreement between Greece, its European partners and the IMF, by which certain fiscal criteria are set as prerequisites for the disbursement of financial assistance, but without blindly imposing policy measures, as currently is the case. The framework of the Maastricht Treaty, or even the frameworks that will be introduced by the European Competitiveness Pact, can be used as blueprints for the new agreement. All decisions regarding policy measures, the amount and type of taxes, which organization should be shut down or how the Public Power Corporation should be reorganized in the years to come, must be reached on the domestic level, and should be judged on the basis of their effectiveness in achieving the set fiscal targets within the agreed deadlines.

In Europe, it is common knowledge that this is the time for more realism and less dogma when reaching decisions that do not concern only the course of an economy, but ultimately society itself. For this reason, the effort for exiting the crisis should be made together with the European Union, as part of a co-decision procedure, characterized by symmetrical responsibility and common goals. It is utterly misleading and damaging when certain 'proud Greeks' lash out against Brussels or Berlin, by denouncing the EU's intervention in Greece's internal affairs. So it is irresponsible when the European authorities or the ECB treat Greece as a basket case, irrespective of governments and policies, in an effort to shake off its own culpability for inaction and indulgence during the past few years, when the Greek economy was crumbling. The contents of this new agreement may include the elements outlined below:

9.3.2. A Realistic Target for Primary Surplus

The primary surplus becomes the cornerstone of fiscal policy, ensuring that all domestic financing needs are covered without any need to resort to new borrowing. In order to be feasible and sustainable, the surplus has to be based on the following premises:

- Efficient collection of taxes, and not the imposition of new ones;
- Containment of government's operating costs, and not new salary and pension cutbacks;
- Use of community resources for boosting the economy, and not for covering short-term expenses, as has been frequently the case in the recent past.

The primary surplus must not provide a springboard for new demands by interest groups or favoured constituencies, as was practised by the distribution of handouts on the eve of European Parliament elections in May 2014. If such tactics are endorsed, they will sweep away any prospect of stabilization. Part of the primary surplus must be used for interest payments, while the remainder for financing growth initiatives and urgent social needs. Markets will start lending Greece again, without any fear of a sovereign default, only when the sustainability and effective use of the primary surpluses can be credibly demonstrated. The best way to safeguard primary surpluses institutionally would be to introduce a constitutional rule that would prohibit any fiscal deficit overshooting the target and would stipulate the mandatory annual reduction of public debt. This is what Spain did in 2011, frustrating the speculators' plans.[5]

9.3.3. Amending the PSI

If the recapitalization of Greek banks continues to be carried out through the European Stability Mechanism, it must take a form that is not burdening public debt. As the amount outstanding today is to the tune of €40 billion, this measure alone would reduce the public debt by almost 25% of GDP, bringing a major immediate relief that would augment any other effort to alleviate debt, thus rendering it more sustainable. One way to do this is by securitizing the preferential shares and using the proceeds to buy Greek sovereign debt in the secondary market.

It would be absurd to use government resources in order to help the banks cover their losses from the impairment of their government bond portfolios, while leaving retail investors to cover their respective losses on their own. Therefore, a solution should also be found for the latter, in a manner that would not establish any legal precedent with regard to banks and large investment funds. The simplest solution is to compensate for this loss through tax credits, which will be extended for as long as required to offset any bond-related losses. This system can work in the manner that tax refunds are handed to farmers and other professionals. Another way is to gradually replace the 'impaired' bonds with Greek Treasury Bills at par, or even to combine the two methods.

9.4. THE INVESTMENT GAP

9.4.1. Recovery Arithmetic

The achievement of 3.50% growth per annum in the medium term requires the realization of an ambitious investment programme. Other growth-enhancing alternatives, such as boosting demand through new loans or generating new incomes by hiring more people in the public sector, are simply non-existent or short-term experiments, at best. The investment programme will speed up the capital accumulation process that the country needs in order to regain growth and acquire a job-creation momentum. The first question is how much investment is needed for this purpose?

The level of investment has to be proportional to the growth rate. As in 2009–2013, investment activity underwent a dramatic contraction and dragged down the growth rate, it now has to be restored along with the recovery of business activity. As shown in Table 9.3, this means that net new investment in the next few years must gradually rise to approximately 10% of GDP, roughly the steady-state level before the crisis. The total amount, that has to be invested by year 2020, stands at €107 billion.

Table 9.3   Restoring Investment Activity in Greece

	GDP, € billion	Net New Investment % of GDP	Net New Investment € billion
2014	184.9	0.67	1.24
2015	192.5	4.52	8.69
2016	201.8	6.82	13.77
2017	211.4	8.21	17.35
2018	221.6	9.04	20.02
2019	232.2	9.53	22.14
2020	243.4	9.83	23.93
Total			**€107 billion**

Note: Required net new investment amounts are compatible with the GDP growth rates described in the alternative debt scenario of Figure 9.1. *Source*: GDP projections from Government Budget 2013/14. Investment shares calculated by the author.

9.4.2. Pick Up the Winners

The second issue is where these funds come from and where will they be channelled to. There have been some interesting studies by specialist organizations, which have identified the productive advantages of each sector in Greece and have estimated the possible investment flows towards them. A recent study is summarized in Table 9.4. The sectors that show the greatest interest for investors include energy, logistics, large-scale tourist facilities, new air transport projects, as well as the restructuring of the companies that were hit hard by the crisis.

These investments also include projects that will be financed through the Community Support Frameworks, as well as various privatizations. In total, expected investment is estimated at €90 billion. This still leaves another €17 billion to be found in order to complete the required total amount of €107 billion. This investment gap can be covered through the establishment of a new growth programme by the European Investment Bank, which will finance infrastructures and new businesses in the countries of the European South and Greece. The recent Juncker investment initiative launched by EU may provide the appropriate framework. But of course, this requires a far-reaching mobilization by competent authorities in Greece and the EU, so as to ensure that the projects to be submitted are feasible and competitive.

This is the only way to restart the economy in an organized manner, restore confidence in the country's potential and create sustainable jobs for the new generation. Otherwise, even if recession subsides in the next year, the country will most probably go through a stage of 'jobless recovery', as businesses will be wary of taking the first signs of growth as an end to uncertainty and will not hire any new personnel.

Only such a framework can simultaneously ensure the recovery of the Greek economy and the sustainability of public debt. Otherwise, the lack of sustained strong growth will keep on causing debt to swell, no matter how

Table 9.4   Required Investments in Greece, by Sector and Source

Category	€ billion
1. Energy connections	12
2. Transport infrastructures	2
3. Tourism infrastructures	3
4. Large-scale tourism units (2025)	20
5. Corporate restructuring	7
6. Current CSF	9
7. Privatization investments	23
8. New CSF	14
Investments, total	**90**
Investment gap 2015–2020	**€17 billion**

Source: Data (1) to (5) from PWC Greece, 2013, *Fuelling Economic Growth in Greece*.
For (7) and (8) data are taken from Ministry of Finance, Greece.

many primary surpluses the government has to show. Uncertainty will hinder any new private investment and the few dollops of recovery will evaporate, without any meaningful effect on employment. Sooner or later, the crisis will come back with a vengeance, making a Grexit seem inevitable.

In order to encourage investment in capital replacement, Greek businesses should be financed at interest rates similar to those applicable in other European countries; such a project can also be jointly undertaken by the European Investment Bank and the ECB. This is how Greek businesses will manage to survive and become competitive in the international market; not through incessant wage cuts, which caused households' incomes to tumble, albeit without restoring competitiveness at all.

9.4.3. Invest and Reform

Rekindling Greece's economy with the aim of reducing debt and unemployment should also be combined with a national plan of reforms, privatizations and the competitive opening up of markets and professions. In the past three years, results have been meagre in these three areas, simply because they were treated as ominous preconditions for receiving the installments of the financial assistance, and not as tools for rebuilding the economy. This way, they provided even the more audacious vested interests with the pretext of flying their standards 'against the foreigners' and employing 'resistance rhetoric' in order to perpetuate their privileges. The reform programme must not be dictated from abroad, so as not to be perceived as just another term of the Memorandums; however, it must contain no favours to partisan and other client groups, which lie in wait in order to resume their precious lobbying and privilege allocation tactics. The programme will provide a structural buttress to the primary surplus and the base for reinstating the reliability of the Greek economy.

If the aforementioned policy proposals are realized in a fast and efficient manner, they would establish favourable conditions for Greece and would enable the country to gradually regain its strategic role both in Europe and the wider region. The accelerating vicious spiral of recession, over-indebtedness and enfeeblement can be curtailed and be replaced by the gradual reinstatement of growth, fiscal sustainability and geopolitical presence. The benefits will not only be felt in Greece, but in the European Union as well. Not just because the prodigal son sobered up and recovered, but also because the fattened calf of the financial assistance did not, after all, go to waste.

In this vein, a series of practical proposals for fast-reforms are presented below. They are not of the grandiose type and will not bring about seismic changes in the country's progress. It should be remembered though, that many high-sounding promises of the past (e.g. the promise to 'remake the state') fell apart because they were ill-prepared and had not, probably, really been owned by those who made them. These proposals mostly aim at establishing an environment that will facilitate the promotion of more reforms in the future, with increased credibility and a greater possibility for success[6]. Critical blocks to this effort are the reform of the tax system, the systematic improvement of fiscal administration, and the consolidation of social cohesion, so as to alleviate uncertainty in the lower-income households.

The proposals can be immediately implemented and, for almost all, sufficient groundwork has been laid in Greece, while lots of experience has been gained from their implementation in other countries.

9.5. A NEW PRIVATIZATION FRAMEWORK

The reform momentum has been defeated and a strong tendency was developed after the 2015 election to reverse even the timid ones that were implemented. Take the privatizations, for example: the fact that the €50 billion privatization package was imposed in 2011 after Troika's repeated demands was exploited by the trade unions to promote the impression that Greece was forcefully put in a 'distress sale', in order to repay its debts. The fact that some privatizations were concluded at lower prices raised several questions regarding the integrity and efficiency of the programme.

The best Greece could do would be to act proactively and carry out certain—though fewer—privatizations, on the basis of its own decisions and policies, in order to be solely responsible for the process and stop giving the impression that it was simply yielding to third-party pressures. For example, the suggestion that public real estate should be used for possible collateralization with Greek debt was a serious setback and triggered a persistent domestic legitimacy crisis. Given that such policies are totally uncommon to be developed, and, in particular, in European economies, the policy suggestions were viewed as resurrecting colonial practices, causing a vehement rejection by public opinion.

In other cases, the reform effort was blocked by the insiders who were tenaciously defending irrational and self-seeking privileges threatened by change. New approaches that will include mutual commitments and predetermined rules regarding the distribution of the anticipated gains are needed, instead of unrealistic calls for rallying around some vague change.

It is absolutely evident that, in order to avoid default and secure the smooth continuation of the repayments programme, business activity must show at least some positive rates, and gradually increase in the forthcoming years. Privatization is one of the few available policies that can not only generate badly needed revenues, but also help restart the economy.

Given the current climate, though, and under the current recessionary conditions, the success of any measures for market development of state property, as well as the privatization of public utility companies (PUCs), is dubious and requires a new careful design and implementation. Both policies are in the right direction, but this is not self-evident. The reason is that, owing to the market's collapse, privatizations cannot generate large revenues, no matter how badly the country needs them.

Setting the privatization target to the overly optimistic level of €50 billion in 2011 may have caused excitement, but made the entire project unfeasible. The exact same thing had happened 20 years ago, when the sweeping—yet slipshod—privatization plans became the alibi for defending state corporatism and thwarted all structural reforms for many years to come. This is why the planned package of privatization policies, state asset divestments and public property development projects should be implemented on the basis of very specific growth targets, instead of merely providing a substitute to the loss of tax revenues. Below are some relevant ideas and proposals, broken down per type of action:

9.5.1. Utilization of State Assets

Taking into account the practices of the past, as well as state property development patterns realized in other countries, the following options can be considered for Greece:

(a) Private partnerships in tourism: In the context of these ventures, the state offers 50-year leases on tourist land, in order to facilitate high-quality and large-scale investments. This arrangement is similar to that applied in the case of Xenia hotels during the 1950s; but now both the financing and

the management will be private. Deals should exclude popular beaches and places of historical interest, in order to avoid the chronic impasse of cases which have been lingering for four decades, precluding any kind of development.

Apart from the initial concession fee, the state would also receive a fixed percentage of incoming profits and keep the right to renegotiate future extensions of the deal. Such arrangements apply in mixed-type property developments that combine housing and soft activities. The prime candidate is the site of the former airport in Athens, before shanties and land-grabbers get a chance to move in.

A similar development model could be used in the case of Olympic Real Estate Company that was established in 2002 with the purpose of staging the Athens Olympics in 2004. After the games, they were expected to generate long-term income through partnerships with private capital and the promotion of sports tourism. Although the change of their use was ratified by the Parliament in 2005, attempts to be sold to private investors were blocked by local authorities who preferred to have access to them for free but declined any participation to their operational cost. Most of the installations are so neglected that they have become rubbish dumps, or are even used as free accommodation for ex-athletes. In October 2014, the management of the company faced criminal charges for neglect, while the property was transferred to the agency for privatization. The process stalled again in 2015.[7]

(b) Urban regeneration: In this case, state land is sold or leased to private investors who in turn undertake the revival and redevelopment of run-down city areas. The aim is to give incentives to new investors to proceed with the demolition of aged urban blocks, and then rebuild them on the basis of cutting-edge environmental and city-planning standards. This option is currently blocked due to the lack of additional space for new uses, and the reluctance of investors to get simultaneously entangled with dozens of small owners and unknown bureaucratic obstacles. The gains in social terms could be huge while possibly no one would protest for abandoned state properties being sold in order to improve zoning conditions in a poor neighbourhood.

(c) Industrial areas: In many regions of Greece the state owns large tracts of land, which can be directly utilized as production facilities, specialized for industry sectors on the basis of comparative advantage and the needs of each region. In the past, many of these tracts had either been encroached on by land-grabbers, or blocked by neighbouring owners, who impeded their development in order to avoid a potential loss in the value of their own properties. The current circumstances have given rise to new opportunities for the development of state lands. The institutional framework is providing the legislation

on establishment, organization and management of industrial parks, although it needs to be enriched with more rigorous technological updates and environmental protection standards. Two areas of specialization are of particular interest for regional development:

(c1) Agro-industry parks: In regions that lack serious productive enterprises, public land could be equipped with basic infrastructures and subsequently used for the establishment of parks exclusively designed for the packaging and distribution of local agricultural products. They may include packaging and standardization facilities, auction houses and light manufacturing units. This way, local producers will be able to sell their goods at more competitive prices, thus improving their income. Moreover, the increase in the added value of the finished goods will contribute to local growth and employment.

(c2) Local energy parks: In regions that suffer from energy shortages, local industrial parks may include extensive renewable energy generation capacity. Subsequently, this can supply greenhouse and hydroponic crops with power. The local economy of many islands can greatly benefit as these projects can provide energy without relying on the costly transfer from mainland power stations. Additionally, they could facilitate and support vital value-added activities, such as desalination, irrigation and small-scale manufacturing.

9.5.2. Privatizing Profitable PUCs

Another area of privatization is the partial or full-scale sale of profitable public utility companies (PUCs). Special attention should also be paid as to whether the privatization of a profitable PUC leads to real new investments and real productivity gains, or merely amounts to a change of ownership. A necessary prerequisite is that competition is enhanced, driving down prices and leading to the improvement of the services provided to consumers. Meeting these criteria is necessary if reforms are going to generate financial gains for the country and, at the same time, enjoy the support of public opinion.

In certain sectors, though, which are considered to be of strategic technological or geopolitical importance, privatizations should be carried out with great care, and without jeopardizing the control and long-term planning of the Greek state. A typical case in point is the energy sector, where the state must retain a decisive stake on strategic issues, in view of the inter-governmental alliances formed in order to influence the new energy markets in the wider region. Hydrocarbon exploration in Greece's territory, the energy negotiations between the European Union and Russia, the oil and gas networks that link South Eastern Europe and the Mediterranean with the Black Sea, give rise to new developments and may lead to major changes in the regional energy map. The energy alliance between Cyprus and Israel, following the discovery of possibly exploitable natural gas reserves in their territorial waters, is a reminder that the state must not forfeit the strategic opportunities that arise.

If the pressure for fast-track privatizations merely leads to the advent of a new private owner, Greece may fail to fully utilize the strategic parameters set in the new energy era. Take the Public Power Corporation (PPC) as an example: fifty percent of the company was privatized during the period 2001–2003, changing its state-organization nature into a profitable modern corporation, perhaps one of the top in South Eastern Europe. Today, the question is how to consolidate Greece's role as a generation, investment and transit hub in the wider region. To this effect, new investment and strategic planning is required, instead of the plain sale of existing power stations, which will result in a mere ownership transfer.

After all, the purpose of the energy market liberalization enacted in 2000 was to attract serious investors who would make new investments in electricity generation, in cutting-edge fields such as natural gas, bio fuels and extensive renewable energy parks. However, if private investors just acquire the existing lignite mines and generation plants, they will not make any new investment. On the contrary, it is possible that output will be scaled down in order that electricity production be auctioned at highest peak rates. In this case, domestic power production will fall short of regular demand and shortages will be covered by electricity imports from neighbouring countries. Such an event may lead to the automatic increase of electricity prices, not only during peak hours, but across the board. As a consequence, this will inevitably increase energy prices, further hitting the Greek industry and competitiveness at large.

9.5.3. Privatizing Loss-making PUCs

Privatization may extend to systematically loss-making PUCs, especially to those that, despite providing expensive and low-quality services, continue to be staffed with surplus employees and run huge deficits. Given that these companies have no access to capital markets, privatization cannot be conducted in market terms but through other financing schemes devised on an *ad hoc* basis.

An example in case is the Hellenic Railways. The company can be leased on a long-term basis to emerging economies (such as China, India, etc.) that are interested in establishing, in the immediate future, transportation and distribution networks in the European market. The gains from such a concession would be twofold: Not only will it stanch the fiscal haemorrhage the corporation is currently running, but it may also generate gains for Greek exports through the expansion of the transportation network. This way, the privatization not only helps fiscally but also improves overall competitiveness.

9.5.4. Overcoming Market Risks

Privatizations should take into account and address a number of shortcomings that may hinder the realization of the programme: First, the prolonged inaction of the past few years has led to a breakdown of communications between the competent authorities and various investment groups interested in privatizations worldwide. Owing to this alienation, re-establishing the country's brand will require lots of preparation and continuous presence in the markets and investors' conferences. This is the only way to ensure that each privatization will not be seen as a 'one-off occurrence', but will be linked to the overall prospects of the Greek economy.

Second, capital markets are weak all over the world, and especially so in Greece. The prices of PUCs listed in the Greek stock exchange are down to few decimal points of their highs during the previous decade. This implies that any stakes disposed of in the stock market would, very possibly, be sold at a heavy discount. To overcome the risk brought about by time pressure on the government to sell quickly in weak markets, a composite and flexible framework for evaluating privatized assets and achieving a satisfactory reduction of public debt is required. Some relevant proposals are considered below:

(a) Purchase of State Property with Discounted Bonds

In 2011, the lenders suggested the creation of a state property fund that would act as national collateral for the bailout loans extended to Greece. The scheme was strongly opposed as a vehicle of expropriating national wealth and soon was abandoned. In its place, the government founded the Hellenic Republic Asset Development Fund (HRADF), to which state assets would be transferred and then put in sale through a coordinated plan.

The Fund was expected to clear the ground for dubious and contested cases of public property, and then return the proceeds to buy off government debt. Though the early ambitions of swift and extensive privatizations remained far from being fully realized, the Fund managed to carry out some thorny privatizations, notably the real estate project at Hellinikon airport in Athens, the Greek Lottery and a few others.

One criticism, however, emerged regarding how exactly the proceeds are used to reduce public debt. The problem arises because both the capital market and the Greek bond market are heavily underpriced. If proceeds are used to buy off debt at face value, the state may incur a loss equal to the capital market discount. One way of overcoming the problem is exchanging proceeds with bonds valued at discounted prices too. Alternatively, investors may first buy the bonds themselves at discount and exchange them for the assets at the purchase price. Thus, state assets are effectively collateralized with public debt but without discount differentials that would have been the case in the initial proposal.

(b) Profit-sharing Agreements

The above arrangement helps avoid the discount caused by a bearish bond market, but is not immune to the possibility of capital markets being bearish for reasons unconnected with the domestic recession. To deal with this, each privatization may also include a clause concerning the partial recovery of future capital gains. For each state holding, a second price will be gradually paid during a time horizon, depending on the increase in the value of the privatized asset.

To increase revenues upfront, the Greek government can issue a security that will be discounting the future capital gains from privatization or exchange it with sovereign bonds in the secondary market.

9.6. A JOBLESS RECOVERY?

Economists tend to think about the relation between GDP growth and changes in unemployment through the so-called Okun's Law, according to which a rise in the former causes a reduction to the latter in a simple linear pattern. In this way, the unemployment hike in Greece is fully explained by the recession after 2009. Symmetrically, a prerequisite for its fall is that the economy recovers and returns to growth. But here lies a potential problem as even if all investments are completed in time and growth is unleashed according to plan, the quick fall in unemployment is far from being ensured.

A report by the European Commission acknowledged that in Greece, 'recession has witnessed a fundamental break in the Greek historical relationship between changes in unemployment and output'.[8] In an analysis that is reproduced in Figure 9.2, the report shows that, before the crisis, Okun's Law was slower, implying that unemployment was only gradually falling with the rise in output. But after the crisis it became steeper, implying that with output falling unemployment surged very quickly.

When recovery eventually returns, unemployment is most likely to change again along the slow pattern. In other words, recession might have been responsible for the massive layoffs and business closures in a matter of four

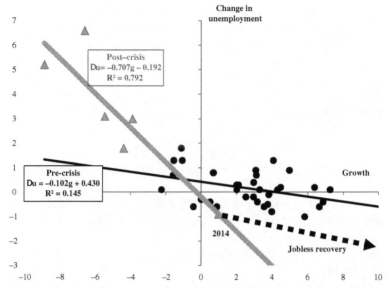

Figure 9.2 The Changing Landscape in the Labour Market. *Note*: (a). 1980–2008: Circles, thin line. (b). 2009–2014: Triangles, thick line. The diagram is based on a similar graph by EC (2013, Box 3, Graph 3.2). *Data source*: Ameco Eurostat. Trend lines obtained by simple regressions.

years, but it is by no means given that if recession is reversed, new jobs will be created at the same speed they were lost. The reason is that increases in employment exhibit a 'hysteresis', that is, they lag behind positive developments in activity as employers are uncertain on the robustness of recovery and refrain from hiring new employees.

This is a stern warning on the possibility that Greece—even after exiting recession—is likely to have a 'jobless recovery' with unemployment still ravaging for years to come. To mitigate the problem, actions that improve the job search and matching process, and facilitate hiring and labour market flexibility should accompany the recovery plan. At the same time, temporary off-market employment schemes in the social sector should be encouraged so as to give to the long-term unemployed an opportunity to get reintegrated into the labour process and then seek full employment elsewhere.

***

Economic recovery and debt sustainability require a wholly different approach to replace the intensity of fiscal consolidation with realistic targets and more growth-oriented policies. A key priority is the recovery of investment activity and this should be supported by privatizations and new business infrastructures. Even if the plan is put on track, there would be two areas that need to be specifically addressed: the first is employment, where more active policies are required to avoid a prolonged hysteresis in new jobs creation; the second is a reform list that should be implemented so as to safeguard fiscal consolidation and promote fairness, as will be examined in the next chapter.

NOTES

1. Debt Sustainability Analysis (DSA) in European Economy, (2013), The Second Economic Adjustment Programme for Greece.

2. OECD, 2013, Economic Surveys: Greece, November, p. 9–10.

3. In January, the yield on the German ten-year, five-year and two-year bond stood at 1.69%, 0.76%, and 0.14%, respectively (data as per 23/1/2014, bloomberg. com/markets/rates-bonds/government-bonds/germany/).

4. For example, if someone has an income of 100 and owes 200, they may think that it is best for them to increase their income by 10 instead of reducing their debt by 10 points through the creation of a surplus. In the former case, the debt accounts for 181% of the income, while in the latter case it accounts for 190%. It is not the same when the debt is low. If, for example, someone with the same income owes 50, it is better to reduce it by 10 points to 40%, than to increase their income to 110 and bring the debt to 45%.

5. A brief description of the reforms adopted in the Spanish Constitution is supplied by Abad and Galante (2011).

6. Let's call these reforms the 'vestibule' of change, as opposed to the proper church, where the liturgy of reform orthodoxy will be held.

7. See relevant reports by Smith (2012) and Papadopoulos (2014).

8. EC (2013, Box 3, p. 11–12).

Chapter 10

A Road Map for Growth

Some Key Fiscal Reforms

The difficulties in introducing market reforms in Greece are discussed first, followed by a list of realistic reforms that should be implemented so as to improve competitiveness and equity in Greece. Suggestions include a fair and more effective tax system, as well as a more reliable control of public expenditure. One of the key proposals is the need for constitutional limits to thwart pre-electoral fiscal sprees that too frequently in the past had accumulated major debt burdens.

10.1. WHY HAVEN'T REFORMS TAKEN ROOT IN GREECE?

Today, it is not anymore at Greece's discretion to choose what to do and what to avoid. It cannot even afford to pick its own pace. It must simultaneously achieve all three targets of re-investment, re-employment and return to growth. Ten years ago, the unwavering decision to join the EMU saved the country from third-world-type debacles. In the same manner today, only the adoption of a new model of dynamic, competitive and balanced growth, replete with structural changes and market reforms, can ensure that Greece will continue to march along with the other European societies, and prevent the fatal divergence and underdevelopment that would possibly occur otherwise. However, Greece shows a high degree of inertia and resistance in taking such a road, and some explanations are needed.

In political theory, there are three approaches that attempt to explain both the conditions under which reforms can be expedited, and the causes of delay in their implementation. These theories are based on the experience of many countries during long periods, and help to understand and explain the slow progress of reforms in Greece.

10.1.1. Adjustment by Regime Change

One approach in the political theory of reform is the so-called 'regime change', which asserts that traditional practices are overturned by the emergence of a new political order. Such phenomena were extensively witnessed in the societies of Eastern Europe after the collapse of communism in the 1990s; in Latin America, following the collapse of the military dictatorships in the 1980s; and more recently in parts of Northern Africa after the ousting of the authoritarian regimes.

In these cases, reform agendas take the political scene by storm, and the public is extremely conducive to their adoption and implementation. However, this happens because citizens hope that reforms will bring about radical changes everywhere; that they will strip the previous order of its prerogatives and create a new set of opportunities, available to wider segments of society. Quite often, though, such hopes fail to materialize, and soon afterwards reforms are met with mistrust and aversion. For example, the societies of Eastern Europe witnessed the creation of new elites by newcomers to politics, but also by officials of the previous regime who were transformed overnight into ardent proponents of free markets. Under the guise of privatizations, they managed to loot state assets in which they participated as both organizers and buyers. Thus, the initial wind of enthusiasm pretty soon changed direction, and many countries preferred to bring back to power parties stemming from the communist legacy of the past, as a way to oppose the new oligarchs formed by converted communists.

But even in case they do have a potent reform agenda, governments are not immune to inertia and de-legitimating when they give the impression that their main concern is to transfer privileges to selected groups, instead of dispersing opportunities throughout the entire range of.

10.1.2. Post-crisis Adjustment

According to this approach, a strong economic shock can become the motive for rapid changes and reforms. If the cost of adjustment is unevenly distributed among the various population segments, those incurring a greater burden will be strongly motivated to bring about changes and overturn the status quo of inaction. This leads to the mobilization of various political forces, which rise above their chronic indecision and set reform as a top priority, in order to overcome the consequences of the crisis as fast as possible and ensure their own survival. Society generously offers its support and consent to those determined to do something practical and effective in order to secure the people's jobs and incomes, as well as the future of their children. This social support is what a government needs to move forward, and this support will by itself generate the necessary consent for further accelerating reform.

Such an example was the political mobilization in Greece, following the currency crisis of 1994. Fearful that a new large devaluation of the drachma would eliminate their purchasing power for many years to come, trade unions adopted more conciliatory positions in regard to public sector reforms required for entering the EMU. In this way, they abandoned their previous anti-reform stance and the government pushed for a realistic Convergence Programme.

A certain prerequisite for that is, however, the existence of a committed government armed with a strong parliamentary majority. Only in this case can the adjustment be utilized in order to reach radical decisions and to start realizing them swiftly. The same rationale applies to the theory of the 'first 100 days', according to which any government with a reform agenda should promote it immediately after it accedes to power, in order to fulfil its pre-election commitments in due time and also have enough time to reap the political benefits of the reforms.

But even when these conditions are met, major difficulties may still emerge when a reform is promoted on the pretext of the economic crisis but without having positive effects in the longer term. Those segments of society that do not benefit from the reform tend to view it as nothing more than temporary measures that some other government will annul as soon as the crisis is over.

The second, and most important, problem is that, while the crisis is looming, an ill-prepared government may reach hasty decisions, without having properly considered the legal aspects, or the political management of the reforms. So, in case any serious problems emerge during their implementation, they may trigger a backlash, jeopardizing the viability of the entire reform effort.

10.1.3. The Forced Adjustment

Finally, a third approach to reform is the so-called 'external enforcement', whereby a country that wants to be part of a supranational entity must complete a series of reforms in order to facilitate its accession and correct any shortcomings.

Other instances occur when a country asks for a bailout or intervention in the currency market to stave off a speculative attack. In this case, the conditionality programme requires a lot harsher policies to be implemented. The organization supplying the relief is usually the International Monetary Fund, and the most widespread programmes were those applied in Latin America economies in the 1980s and 1990s to harness hyperinflation and excessive deficits. Their policy recommendations reflected the neo-liberal economic orthodoxy of the time code named as the 'Washington Consensus'.[1] Five key policies were included in the prescription:

a. Tight monetary policy to combat inflation
b. Front-loaded austerity to cut fiscal deficits
c. Extensive market deregulation
d. Drastic wage cuts to improve competitiveness
e. Quick privatization of strategic sectors

The blueprint was designed to be common to all cases without taking into account specific conditions or setting priorities on how policies should be implemented. The front-loaded character was usually causing further recession, uncertainty was magnified rather than dissipated and society was ravaged by new and extensive inequalities. Nobel Laureate Joseph Stiglitz launched a famous polemic against such programmes by arguing that:

> the net effect of policies set by the Washington Consensus has all too often been to the benefit of the few at the expense of the many, the well-off to the expense of the poor. In many cases, commercial interests and values have superseded concern for the environment, democracy, human rights and social justice.[2]

In practice, most countries continued to run severe economic imbalances and were soon entrapped in explosive debt processes and a new phase of serial collapsing.

10.1.4. Greece's Experience

Greece has mostly experienced situations related to the latter two theories. The regime change that took place in 1974 after the collapse of the military dictatorship and the restoration of democracy gave rise to many institutional initiatives, but hardly any that could be ranked as competitive market reform. If anything, economic changes were in the direction of nationalizing some private banks and large companies, rather than enhancing competition and market liberalization. At the same time, the return and expansion of civil liberties led to a strong trade-union movement that struggled to achieve a more fair distribution and end political and social exclusions.

The second approach of post-crisis adjustment is more relevant with the experience of reforms in Greece, but mainly to explain why they didn't work due to the lack of governments committed to reforms or the tactics of their successors to unfold previous policies. Take, for example, the Stabilization Programme of 1985. Several of the reforms were repealed two years later, along with the Programme itself, by the very government that had introduced it. Another example concerns the reforms that were introduced after 1990, when a fiscal and economic crisis was looming large. Most of these reforms were also repealed after 1994, when a new government was elected. Similar repeal zeal has been exercised by the left-wing government since the 2015 elections.

Some argue that, in crisis situations, a coalition government that comprises many political forces has more potential. They obviously assume that this would reduce partisan opposition and would facilitate the wider acceptance of the reforms; nonetheless, it ignores the fact that if coalition governments are not internally coherent and do not demonstrate a uniform zeal for promoting change, they may reduce resoluteness and coordination, instead of enhancing them. A dramatic case in point is when, in 1989, two coalition governments were formed in order to deal with the crisis of that time, but the economy collapsed anyway within six months, as nobody wanted to bear, or be seen to be sharing, the cost of inescapable decisions. Hence, each coalition partner passed the buck to the others, leading to a complete stalemate.

A more recent manifestation was the coalition government formed after the elections in June 2012 by the conservative party, socialists and the party of Democratic Left. The first of them had to reverse its previous rhetoric against austerity and did so at the cost of minimizing reforms damaging its favourite constituencies in the public sector. The socialist party was decimated in the polls, falling from 43% to just over 8% of the vote. Striving to stave off further losses, it adopted a soft line too. The third party was set against public sector dismissals, and when the deficit-prone National Television was shut down, the coalition broke down. The government continued as a two-party coalition, but several reforms were subsequently shelved to avoid further backlash.

The third approach of the 'forced adjustment' is even more relevant if one wishes to explain the uneven progress of reforms. It is quite revealing for one to see that most of the reforms occurred a few years before or after the country's entry to the Economic and Monetary Union. The reforms in the structure of the financial and banking systems, in fiscal policy, taxation, state enterprises, and, to a much lesser extent, in the labour market and the social security system, mainly occurred under the influence, and as part of the enforcement, of the Maastricht criteria.

Even this process, though, was neither straightforward, nor automatic. Despite the fact that the Maastricht Treaty had been voted for by the vast majority of Greek Parliament, the political forces did not appear to be equally committed to the consensual promotion of the necessary reforms, in order to achieve swift compliance with the criteria and ensure Greece's unimpeded accession to the Economic and Monetary Union. It took a succession of elections and many revisions of the Convergence Programme to expedite reform in key areas, which finally led Greece to join the EMU.

There were, nonetheless, two elements, which made reform more feasible: first, the totally binding deadline of year end 1999, which had been set as the ultimate date for complying with the criteria; otherwise Greece would have to wait to become an EMU member at some unspecified later stage. Second, the resources of the Community Support Framework, which financed a substantial part of the growth effort, were set to be conditional on tangible progress in regard to the convergence criteria. In turn, economic growth raised positive expectations of employment and prosperity. This at the same time made it easier to 'compensate' those groups that were hurt by the reforms, through pension benefits, salary increases (as in the case of public sector organizations and enterprises slated for privatization) and investment incentives.

With the advent of the 2008 crisis, certain quarters in Europe believed that it was once again time for external reform enforcement. The international crisis would impose a framework for managing the economy more effectively, which, in turn, would catalyse a new reform dynamic. In Greece, this approach was articulated by the Memorandum as a condition for the provision of the financial assistance. Its rigid timetable and the far-reaching requirements it involved were hailed as the roadmap for reform in Greece.

Compared, though, with the tight deadlines of the EMU, the constraints of the Memorandum were different in two important ways:

One reason was that the EMU conditionality, which corresponded to a reform framework that had been discussed at length in Greece, was similarly implemented in other states with more enviable living standards, and offered great national discretion in regard to the policy mix required for complying with the accession criteria. This ensured the domestic political legitimization of reforms rather than being a dictation from abroad as mostly happened with the Memorandum.

The main reason, however, was that in its way to EMU the economy was experiencing a rapid growth with new opportunities for employment and higher living standards open to all. This led to the formation of a concrete set of widely accepted changes. In contrast, the Memorandum led the economy to a state of deep recession, massively reducing the living standards and exacerbating inequalities. The unequal distribution of reform costs amplified the pressures exerted by the crisis on many social groups, and thus the whole programme was fiercely resisted by a variety of social groups. For example, private sector employees were against the programme because it was insisting on measures facilitating their dismissals, while at the same time overly protecting public sector employment. Civil servants were even more aggressive because the programme introduced private-sector assessment criteria for their promotion. Both groups were protesting the wage cuts.

Somehow the two prerequisites of a growth perspective and national ownership of the reform programme have to be recovered, for the agenda to be likely to succeed. A new agreement that promotes growth and leaves the elected to choose the programme of reforms conditional on achieving certain fiscal targets is more likely to succeed than if dictated on every detail by outside authorities. To this effect, a number of reform proposals are outlined below. The proposals aim at more fairness and effectiveness, so that they may avoid the handicaps of previous reform efforts. They are simple in their description so that they are easily communicated and assessed, rather than complicated plans which so many times in the past have been cancelled just after taking off.

10.2. TAX REFORMS

The Greek tax system is a key factor in preventing an adequate and sustainable fiscal consolidation. The main reasons for its ineffectiveness are the complexity and continuous variation of tax rules, and the weak capacity of revenue collection.

Complexity and variations are the cumulative outcomes of incessant political interventions that—more often than not—view the tax system as the ultimate tool to magically amend all other deficiencies of economic and social policies. In the past, tax exemptions and special provisions had been repeatedly used for supporting income in certain ailing sectors or powerful lobbies, to promote social equity or for smoothing out regional inequalities; and sometimes even as a complementary wage policy by differentiating tax treatment of various benefits in the public sector. Gradually, this led to the creation of a system that is complex, abstruse and difficult to implement. The administrative costs are huge but, nevertheless, its impact is impossible to assess. Moreover, provisions change at least as frequently as political parties alternate in power, sometimes even after a government reshuffle.

A simple system containing stable tax regulations, as well as effective mechanisms for settling disputes with tax authorities could not be more urgently needed. Especially amid recession, households become even more uncertain with the imposition of new emergency taxes looming large on the horizon, and no business can recover if it feels constantly exposed to retroactive tax amendments. The bitter lesson of previous years is that the mobilization to raise revenues should not be conducted by imposing new burdens on those who have been properly paying their dues, but by the systematic taxation of those avoiding doing so.

Below are some measures that may help to raise efficiency and effectiveness by improving the allocation of tax burden, while, at the same time, boosting the badly needed revenues. Some of them were enacted by the Tax Reform in 2003, though not applied for long as most of its provisions were withdrawn by the government elected in March 2004.

10.2.1. Uniform Tax Treatment

A modern fiscal administration must get rid of many discriminatory, unfair, industry-specific or local-specific tax regulations and exemptions. Any remaining social or development priorities that possibly (or just potentially) justified them in the past should be directly financed through explicit budget allocations, so that a better evaluation of their impact is obtained. This will immediately reveal to parliamentary control, as well as to the wider public, how much money is effectively allocated to each entity, and for what purpose.

For example, how much do taxpayers pay for footballers who enjoy a special tax treatment; how much do they subsidize an institution which is vested with tax exemptions; or what tax breaks are given to various professional groups; things that, up to now, remain hidden in obscure regulations that few are aware of, even fewer understand, and nobody reviews. As soon as these things become known, the public will be faced with such an absurd landscape of tax favouritism that will help to attract political support in abolishing it. A case in point is the regional differentiation of the VAT system, by which the Aegean islands are granted lower rates as compensation for higher transportation costs. Though some of them are characterized by the highest per capita income in Greece, tax exemptions continue unabated and previous attempts to unify rates were resisted by local lobbies.

10.2.2. Targeted Tax Hikes

In most economies, tax revenues follow an asymmetric pattern: tax rate cuts lead to a roughly proportional reduction in tax revenues. Tax hikes, though, are not translated to a proportional rise in revenues as avoidance increases. The propensity of tax avoidance is stronger in a recession, not only because disposable incomes are strained but also as a means to increase liquidity and working capital by small firms and professionals.

In 2010, the government tried to make certain professionals pay some tax by imposing a 23% VAT rate on lawyers, plumbers, etc. Then, it sat back and waited for a new stream of revenues, but, as shown in chapter 4, they were actually reduced! The problem was precisely the high VAT rate. Consider that the VAT rate is set at 23% and the income tax rate at 45%. If a client has to pay a €1,000 fee to a lawyer and asks for a receipt, payment increases by another €230, an amount that usually is considered prohibitively high and the request is abandoned. Thus, the government loses €230, plus another €450 from undeclared income tax—a total of €680 loss in revenue.

Let's suppose now that the VAT rate is set at a minimal level of 4%. The client would probably be more willing to pay €40 in order to see the lawyer bear part of the tax burden. In this case, the government would collect €40 plus €450 from declared income—a total of €490. Therefore, if the government wishes to close in upon the professionals who do not issue receipts, the best solution is to set a lower VAT rate, instead of a high one.

10.2.3. Offshore Activities

Another area in which further tax monitoring is required regards offshore activities. Thousands of offshore companies are operating in Greece, having a single real-estate property as their only asset. Large areas in high-end suburbs of Athens and cosmopolitan islands seem to be registered in tax havens, helping to avoid the payment of a substantial part of the property taxes that should be normally paid. After the implementation of the austerity programme, a large number of businesses also went offshore to enjoy lower rates and less auditing, thus cutting the tax base in Greece. Offshore real-estate companies are taxed by a special property tax, which is now set at adequate levels. Offshore firms are a more difficult catch. One way to penalize their activity and press them to move back to Greece would be to prohibit their participation in any kind of public procurement projects financed by the Greek state or through EU programmes.

10.2.4. Point System in Tax Audits

In order to fight corruption practices, the 2003 Tax Reform provided for the implementation of a tax auditing process, whereby the levying of fines was to be performed by separate departments. This measure aimed at abolishing the discretion of imposing fines by the tax auditor, so as to reduce the incentives for collusion. Instead, a point system was introduced to penalize the firm in case it is found to break the rules. According to this system, the audit team submits a report, but does not specify any fines or penalties. The report is forwarded to a separate department, which is not organically linked to any audit team. Fines are imposed only after a certain threshold of penalty points is reached, while the same team never performs successive audits in the same business and certainly not before a period of time has elapsed. The system was abolished in 2005 without any prior assessment. After so many failures in reforming corporate taxation, reinstating the point system is perhaps the only way to restore confidence and reduce offshore company registration.

10.2.5. Simplification

When people talk about tax reform in Greece, they usually refer to the increase or decrease of tax rates. However, the experience of other developed countries has shown that simplicity of rules and transparency of regulations are much more important factors than reductions in tax rates for boosting efficiency. Easy as it may seem, simplification may be the most challenging change in the tax system. Bureaucracy is usually united against simplification out of fear of losing the control it currently exercises through the derivation and implementation of complex rules. Resistance will also come from a multitude of lobbies formed by accountants, tax consultants and lawyers, whose profitable expertise currently lies in explaining and managing exactly this complexity of the current system.

10.2.6. Collection Efficiency

On top of other inefficiencies, complexity of tax rules has the effect of making the collection mechanism even more bureaucratic and difficult to be assessed on a results basis. Too much activity is wasted on interpreting the rules, and this makes tax disputes to perpetuate and new evasive practices to be considered. Thus, simplification will by itself enhance collective capacity and allow the mechanism to concentrate on the revenue target on which its performance can be assessed.

But this is hardly enough anymore. Decades of discretionary interpretation of tax rules has created extensive links between the administration and the political system. Tax authorities are regularly replaced at any government change or even after a ministerial reshuffle. In the past, it was not uncommon to see high ranking tax officials to have so close party affiliations that they have even been candidates for various elected government posts in the same constituencies as the ones where they were responsible for tax collection. Eventually, this became so embarrassing that in 2000 the government passed a law prohibiting tax executives from holding political positions with the local government administration in the same jurisdiction as the tax authority for which they worked.[3] Moreover, regional and national tax auditing centres were established so the cases are handled by more centralized authorities. These structures were cancelled after the 2004 elections and absorbed again by the decentralized bureaucracy where local political intervention was more accessible.

As efficient tax collection was a key concern of the austerity programme— and one of the few being fully justified to insist on—the government conceded to appoint a professional on a five-year tenure to manage the revenue mechanism. It was only a matter of time before the outside expert became a political scapegoat and was forced to resign after the disappointing results in the 2014 European elections.

To avoid such backlashes in the future, a solution would be to make the tax mechanism an independent authority vested with constitutional guarantees against political interference. Its head should be appointed—on a par with ministerial status—by a qualified majority in Parliament for a prescribed time period and assessed on actual outcomes. Simplification of rules, tax reforms and institutional autonomy are the only possible combination that can credibly carry out the much-needed consolidation of public revenues.

10.3. CONSTITUTIONAL REFORMS

The other factor that has repeatedly frustrated the efforts of fiscal consolidation is the absence of institutional guarantees that spending controls will be respected without being overturned by opportunistic tactics. Such practices thrive on the eve of elections as a way to appeal to pressure groups. They are also exercised through a widespread network of unstoppable remuneration claims and litigations by the public sector unions. Court rulings are often in support of retroactive pay compensations, including the salaries of the judges themselves. The only way to establish credible rules on public expenditure is by national constitutional provisions or supranational procedures in the Eurozone.

The incorporation of financial rules and fiscal constraints into constitutional charters is the exception rather than the rule in developed nations. The subject of constitutional fiscal rules came up in the United States a few decades ago, as a means for constraining the government's ability to resort to large deficit spending and borrowing in response to the stagflation of that time. In practice, they were adopted by several US states as a means of containing excessive fiscal expansion, which could otherwise cause the federal deficit to swell and lead to an increase in taxation throughout the entire country.

10.3.1. The Eurozone Fiscal Rules

Initially, constitutional rules were severely criticized as fiscal collateral requirements of monetarist policy, and therefore were not popular at all in regard to the agenda of European politics. The most well-known example is probably Germany's national obsession with low inflation, which was officially enacted into law in 1952 as an antidote against the risk of repeating the hyperinflation episode of the 1920s, with its dire consequences. Many things have changed since then, however.

First of all, the Maastricht Treaty set a number of fiscal criteria that member states had to adhere to in each year, both in the run-up to their accession to the EMU and during its operation. Along the way, the lax implementation of these criteria made the Stability and Growth Pact, as the set of rules came to be known, to appear as ineffective in restraining the spending propensity of member states. The fact that the Eurozone was taken by surprise when the debt crisis broke out in 2009 and 2010, necessitated the introduction of the Fiscal Compact. Put into operation in 2013, it provides for more detailed procedures in regard to the implementation of fiscal policy and the assessment of its impact in each member state.

In 2011, Spain introduced fiscal rules into its constitution, thus reinforcing its credibility as a country capable of achieving fiscal stabilization on its own, without requiring any externally imposed programme. The markets responded positively and Spain was spared the ordeal of seeking a bailout agreement with the IMF and the European institutions. Similar initiatives were later considered in Italy for the same reason, though no specific amendments are yet implemented.

10.3.2. Electoral Profligacy

Moreover, academic research in many countries revealed that incumbent governments often attempt to sway the outcome of an impending election by various economic interventions. These are applied either through direct fiscal measures of handouts and tax credits as a last ditch attempt to please undecided households, or by means of dubious decisions and practices that effectively favour politically affiliated groups and vested interests. Both actions incur direct or indirect fiscal costs. Sometimes they reach such a degree of fiscal profligacy that they *de facto* deprive the new government of policy instruments that are essential for fulfilling its own commitments (the so-called 'scorched earth' policy).

In chapter 1, the political cycle in Greece was shown to be characterized by both rise in expenditure and fall in revenue in many election years, while the climate of misgovernance and neglect that prevailed before the elections created opportunities for bending the law without consequences. The list of pre-electoral concessions may also include stretching or changing existing laws so as to directly favour potential supporters. The most common are the extensive pardoning of traffic fines; the increase of *numerus clausus* in tertiary education; and the announcement of new universities in marginal constituencies. In the past, favours included mass hiring in the public sector without entry qualifications, or even lowering threshold criteria for easier promotion of those already within the administration.

The consequences of the electoral cycle are costly both in terms of fiscal deterioration as well as institutional derailment. If fiscal costs are not immediately dealt with, effects will escalate and form a permanent burden on public finances. For example, the electoral cycles of 1980–1981 and 1989–1990 resulted in abysmal deterioration of public deficits and led to prolonged periods of instability. Scars are left even if such consequences are dealt with, albeit by means of universal austerity measures, instead of directly cancelling the favour and burdening only those who profited from it. This may result in higher inequalities and generalized recession. The case in point is, of course, the electoral cycle of 2009 and its aftermath.

Dubious pre-election actions not only generate fiscal costs, as described above, but also harm the equality of citizens before the law, which is supposed to be the keystone of all constitutions. Indiscriminate fiscal consolidation violates the principle that each citizen contributes according to their own responsibilities and ability. Therefore, the establishment of rules designed to prevent fiscal excesses is the best way for effectively upholding the main tenets of the Constitution. Rules that would constrain or prevent such practices are constitutionally legitimate and socially indispensable. Invoking the principle of equality before the law also provides the motive for reviewing other actions, which also generate substantial fiscal costs that, quite often, cannot be timely predicted or easily absorbed. In order to inform and mobilize citizens about the need for constitutional provisions, it is critical that the Budget Office of the Greek Parliament presents regular estimates of the fiscal cost generated by ostensibly non-fiscal arrangements endorsed by the legislature.

To the same effect, constitutional rules may stipulate that underwriting of loans granted to PUCs with a government guarantee are authorized by Parliament on a case-by-case basis, and are not left to the discretion of ministries. Moreover, no cost overrides will be allowed in the case of ongoing public works without parliamentary approval and public notification.

10.3.3. Corporatist Court Rulings

Another loophole that has to be constitutionally addressed is the fact that fiscal policy is frequently frustrated by court rulings regarding remuneration scales in the public sector. After a new benefit is introduced for a specific category of civil servants, there is a serial claim by trade unions to be extended to other categories, no matter if they actually qualify for it. More often than not, Greek courts award retroactive salary increases or find that pay cuts had not been imposed legally and should be reimbursed. Other rulings concern the earnings of the judiciary and it is no wonder that all such decisions are issued to their own favour. The fiscal cost incurred is very serious and may further multiply as a new wave of claims follows suit. An attempt by the government to deal with the problem by establishing a Salary Tribunal made it even more complicated: the tribunal was once again staffed by regular judges who immediately resumed the same practices.

Apart from the fiscal cost, this practice raises embarrassing questions regarding the separation of powers in a democratic system: by means of its salary-related rulings, the judiciary redefines the law passed by the legislature for public sector wages. At the same time, it interferes with the outcomes of fiscal policy implemented by the executive. During the implementation of the austerity programme, courts overruled several wage and pension cuts, thus making stabilization efforts even more difficult and inequitable.

10.3.4. Curbing Abuses in Public Administration

Another recurring factor boosting public expenditure is the propensity of governments to make clientelistic appointments of superfluous and usually unqualified personnel, by circumventing the certified selection procedure. Even if detected later, it is most likely that ill-appointed staff finds a way to continue unabashed and keep collecting a salary. The tenure that accompanies patronage hires constitutes a major flaw of Greece's public administration and evolves in the following way: once a person is appointed in the public sector he or she is invested with certain rights and privileges that effectively inhibit dismissal. Even the most egregious illegality is considered to be 'instant', and there is no practical room for its reversal *ex post*.

A public outcry broke out in the 1990s, when it was discovered that dozens of employees had been hired by a large state organization as engineers, by presenting forged university degrees. Since their job description and placement had been officially approved afterwards and the forgers had been allocated tasks, not only were they not dismissed as frauds, but continued to collect the same salaries assigned to qualifications that they never possessed. In 2013, the government decided several dismissals of incompetent personnel, but the action has not been finalized and was stalled by the new government elected in 2015.

The flexibility of task allocation after the appointment and the lax attitude towards qualifications are exploited by many civil servants who try to move to other positions through internal transfers. In this way they avoid the competition they would endure if the intended post was publicly contested. Under this relocation framework, low skilled employees seek to move to administrative posts, those with outside tasks to office work, and almost everybody to the Ministry of Finance to get the high pay differential. Several critical posts in remote areas are left unstaffed as appointees manage to be quickly relocated at a place closer to their home address. Much of this mobility is orchestrated by the political parties and members of government, since they are entitled to appoint civil servants as aides. The internal reallocation system has become so clientelistic and extensive that it has incapacitated a substantial part of civil administration.

One way to put an end to such practices is to impose the obligation that each one serves the position that they are appointed for. In case that civil servants believe that they deserve a better position they have to compete on an equal basis with any other interested for the same post. The ban will immediately result in three types of benefits:

i. Remote public agencies will not be deserted and thus may provide better services to citizens; for example, medical centres in islands or in border areas.
ii. Outsiders from the private sector will have an equal opportunity to compete for a civil service post rather than being excluded by dubious insider schemes.
iii. The incessant interaction with political patronage will be eliminated, and public administration may have a real opportunity of becoming more efficient and dedicated.

10.3.5. New Constitutional Provisions

Based on the above, it is obvious that a constitutional revision needs to include new provisions in regard to the following:

i. The establishment of annual limits for fiscal deficit and debt increases, with special emphasis on the permissible levels during election years. The constraints can be lifted only in the case of a major crisis or war by a specially qualified majority.
ii. The prohibition of enacting any kind of expansionary policy (e.g. hires, salary increases, etc.) during election years. If such policies have already been passed by Parliament and snap elections are announced, their provisions are automatically revoked in order to be reconsidered after the election. Unlawful and unqualified appointments in the public sector should be fully cancelled retroactively.
iii. The establishment of basic fiscal rules regarding the operation of public bodies outside the central government (e.g. municipalities, regional administrations, public utilities, etc). This will reduce the propensity to run deficits through expansionary policies and perks for their staff, and then passing on the costs to the taxpayer.
iv. The abolition of the courts' power to overturn the remuneration scales of public servants on a massive scale. Any disputes and claims shall be referred to extrajudicial arbitration institutions or European bodies.

***

A number of fiscal reforms have been described that would improve revenue collection, harness public expenditure and curb current abuses. Having achieved fiscal credibility, Greece could push ahead by establishing new rules for banking and investment activities so that the risk of previous malpractices is minimized as examined in the next chapter.

NOTES

1. See Williamson (1990).
2. Stiglitz, *Globalization and its discontents* (2002, p. 20).
3. Article 16 of law 28730, ratified in 2000. For details on the institutional laxity of the Greek tax system, see Skouras and Christodoulakis (2014).

Chapter 11

The Feasible Prosperity

A New Contract for Greece

After the crisis, new regulations are needed for the banking sector and a new social contract should be reached between corporations, the state and citizens. A key reform is with regard to the social security system aiming to increase its long-term viability, as well as to enhance equity among generations. This chapter proposes a system of universal rules on social insurance, according to which pensions, state co-financing and benefits would be universally proportional to actual contributions. A fractional incorporation of hitherto benefits is proposed so as to safeguard the so-called 'established advantages' by the insiders but terminate their continuation in the future.

11.1. THE STATE AND THE ECONOMY

The lesson Greece has painfully learnt from the crisis is that she can neither base its prosperity on the constant inflow of fleeting transfers or loans from abroad, nor by selling land and real estate to foreigners as widely practised in the years of the boom. More than any other European country, Greece will need to reorganize its productive base in order to be able, in the forthcoming years, to achieve higher added value; raise employment and living standards; increase international competitiveness to heal its chronic external deficits; and facilitate reforms and technological improvements to replace outdated structures and practices.

This pursuit will shake traditional roles, and new relationships among businesses, markets and the state shall emerge. The state must be the first to trust private enterprise and stop seeing businesses and their profits as a 'necessary evil', worthy only of taxation. It should facilitate investments, not only the few large ones, but primarily the many small ones that streamline production, create jobs and improve competitiveness.

Today, the public administration's response to the calls for simplifying licensing and investment procedures has been negligible. In many cases, firms are faced with even greater delays, resulting from the perennial reticence of the bureaucracy, the frequent interruptions in the operation of state agencies and their inadequate staffing—itself the result of continuous personnel transfers. Recently, the unwillingness that civil servants often show, aims at frustrating the government's initiatives as payback for the salary cuts they have suffered through the austerity programme. Moreover, tax uncertainty and variability discourage business from designing crisis-exit strategies. Several firms have cancelled investment plans, since any financial activity may turn them into potential tax-evasion suspects and prospective subjects of never-ending audits.

The competitive advantage of the business sector and the market is that they can generate ideas, produce goods and create employment. The competitive advantage of the state is that it can make interventions and finance infrastructures that no one else would do, as well as supervise and control capital movements and placements. Based on this simple comparative advantage theory, we can produce a new state-economy mix, which will respond to the needs of the future and avoid any repetition of past excesses.

Redefining the contours between the state and the markets after the 2008 crisis is an exercise that is neither univocal nor predetermined. After the 1929 crisis, most developed economies and, gradually all other economies, moved on to a phase of intensive state intervention at all levels of economic activity. During the 1987 crisis, though, which was also caused by an extensive collapse of the financial system, the response was quite the opposite. In the post-stagflation years, it was deemed imperative to move the state *out* of mainstream economic activity, while the free market philosophy enjoyed unprecedented acceptance almost everywhere. It is indeed telling that when the efforts for establishing the EMU began around that time, all the entry criteria that were laid down concerned the containment of state activity—not a single one was about the performance or obligations of the private sector. The convergence criteria requested that public deficit is kept below 3% of GDP; public debt sufficiently approaches 60% of GDP; the exchange rate is kept within a narrow band of fluctuations up to 2–25%; while 10-year-bond yields and inflation rates deviate by only a little amount from the best performing indicators among other member states. Of all these criteria, only the inflation rate is primarily linked to the private sector behaviour: the other fall strictly in the obligations of the public sector.

Only in the aftermath of the financial crisis of 2000 and the bursting of the tech bubble, did some serious measures, aimed at the supervision of business behaviour, start being taken in order to moderate the excesses of financial greed.

The current crisis will lead again to a redefinition of the role of the state and, in general, the public sector. But, however much the economy needs to distance itself from the recent unfettered operation of markets it also needs to shun any nostalgia for the statist past that has been singularly unsuccessful in driving the economy forward. A new balance needs to be struck that promotes prosperity without threatening it with excessive debt; supervises markets without suffocating them; and creates business opportunities instead of suppressing them.

A redefinition of the economic role of the state is based on two pillars: the first concerns the consequences of the austerity programme on the financial system and, in particular, the banks. As their recapitalization to compensate for the losses they incurred from cutting public debt holdings in 2012 was financed by new public debt, the state (through the Hellenic Financial Stability Fund) appears now to be effectively the main shareholder. It would be wrong if the government exploited these irrational practices with the aim of creating a new banking sector under state control. One should always remember that as the financial system failed to control the misguided practices of the recent decades that led to the crisis, so did the state fail in the 1970s and the 1980s to control the voracious bureaucracy and the patronage networks imposed on it by the clientelistic political system.

The second pillar of state intervention concerns the rekindling of economic growth. Once again, a distinction has to be made between horizontal state support and discretionary government intervention. The former is a prerequisite for businesses to reorganize their competitive advantage and maintain employment levels. The latter would only serve certain interest groups that exploit their influence over the ownership of this business, just to make sure that new jobs will be allocated by partisan criteria. Instead of nationalizing banks and other private business, it would be much more helpful for all stakeholders to create new jobs and new activities, by establishing those infrastructures that will not only accelerate the exit from the crisis but at the same time create competitive advantages when the crisis is over.

11.2. CORPORATE RESPONSIBILITY AND GOVERNANCE

Corporate governance was introduced in Greece in the early 2000s, in an effort to restore the shareholders' trust in corporations, especially large ones, the value of which had been reduced to less than half in the years following the bursting of the dotcom bubble in 2000.

The model was then adopted by many companies, both private and public. However, it was more of a successful institutional exercise, and rather less of a concrete institutional procedure, capable of overhauling corporate behaviour and dubious practices. The concept of corporate social responsibility (CSR) also started to gain popularity during that period; however, it never became a point of wide societal attention.

The same happened again with the global crisis of 2008. In the aftermath of the crisis and in the wake of several corporate scandals worldwide, concerted practice and anti-consumer behaviour, perhaps this is a chance to redefine the principles of corporate governance and responsibility, combining them to address such problems.

The loss of confidence to the financial system and the consequent collapse of many companies require a major redefinition of disclosure rules and practices in order for trust to be re-established among business, employees and society at large. Take, for example, the companies of the financial sector. Shareholders were not the only ones to sustain losses by placing their funds in toxic investment firms. The same happened to small depositors, who, at a very low interest rate, placed their savings in a bank and saw them being jeopardized. That was not because the bank's deposit strategy failed, but because the financial institution engaged in risky investment behaviour, which was not properly disclosed to retail shareholders and customers. The latter should have been informed about the risks that, without their own knowledge and consent, the bank had assumed by making dubious placements or recklessly evaluating its own assets.

At the same time, this is an opportunity for a more profound reconsideration of issues pertaining to the performance and evaluation of executives. Instead of using complex criteria of management evaluation—the cornerstone of corporate governance—it would be preferable to consider imposing more transparent commitments and responsibilities on bank and business executives. For example, why shouldn't executives pledge their own assets as collateral guarantee against the possibility of a collapse in the value of the business? Or, why shouldn't executives be prohibited from exercising their stock options for a long period following their departure from the company? Such measures, which actually link the executives' personal assets to the fate of the company, may prove to be much more effective than most rhetoric by corporate governance specialists.

Finally, a major issue in the relationship between business and society at large is how to deal with various cases of corruption, from the bribing of executives to overcharging and unfair practices against other businesses. Finally, a thorny issue concerns the accumulation of a 'corruption deposit' on the country's reputation, which if not effectively dealt with, is going to exist there for many years to come.

Apart from litigations, another way of dealing with this is to activate various corporate supervision mechanisms, such as the Capital Market Commission.

This action was implemented by the US Securities and Exchange Commission (SEC) in regard to major corporate scandals. The main argument of the SEC was that corrupt practices violated the Exchange Act, thus misguiding and, ultimately, causing damage to investors, shareholders of other companies, and society at large.[1] Greek capital market legislation, as amended in 2004, contains provisions similar to those of the United States, and could be used for dealing with business scandals, beyond and above the jurisdiction of other institutions.[2]

11.3. A NEW ROLE FOR BANKS

The Greek banking system can play a key role in the formation and financing of the new growth effort. It had done so in the past, though not always in the most effective manner. Quite often it was wary of supporting dynamic new ventures, but would happily secure the re-financing of an existing company that it came to know through social and political connections. In the previous decades, Greek banks also participated in programmes aimed at supporting 'state-subsidized' entrepreneurship in age-old industries, instead of channelling available funds to new investments solely on the basis of international competitiveness, quality and exports.

In spite of shortcomings and pitfalls in the past, the Greek banking system eventually managed to achieve some definite tasks. In the run-up to the EMU, many banks were merged and restructured in order to adapt to the new single currency environment; as a result, not only did they avoid being threatened by the rapid fall of interest rates, but also managed to exploit the process for consolidating their presence in Greece and abroad. At that time, Greek banks boasted a large presence in foreign markets, with branches and executives in fifteen European, Asian and African countries. Though cutting their portfolios abroad after the PSI, Greek banking presence abroad is still the best driver for attracting foreign investments in Greece, a key prerequisite for new comparative advantages and sustainable growth.

Greek banks nevertheless succumbed—admittedly by far less than the banks of other countries—to the frenzy of extending consumer loans to households that were unable to repay them, fuelling the dream of living a good life beyond their actual means. They also yielded to the temptation of giving bonuses proportionally to the quantitative increase of turnover, but not always based on strict criteria of sustainability and risk mitigation.

Initially, Greek banks coped with the 2008 crisis much better than the banks of other countries. They remained almost unscathed by the storm that caused the collapse or dramatic capital impairment of several historic banks in the United States and Northern Europe. Greek pension funds were not hurt by any loss-making investments of Greek banks,[3] whereas the opposite was true even of Scandinavian countries (e.g. Iceland), which are traditionally more careful than the European South in regard to risk management. Thus, when the global crisis broke out, Greek banks did not collapse as in other countries and deposits were not put in any danger. Assisted by the ECB, they turned their government bond holdings into a vital liquidity instrument, which they used for financing businesses and households, in order to help them avoid the effects of the looming recession.

Even the injections of state capital into Greek banks in 2008 were mostly a proactive measure, instead of being a response to problems caused by the crisis, and could have been much more limited. In the period of Memorandum when the Greek state had been cut off from international markets, the Greek banks held very successful rights issues, demonstrating their own dynamism, as well as the long-term capabilities of the Greek economy. Then the PSI came, dealing a blow to their assets and necessitating a new capitalization at a much larger scale.

As it stands today, the Greek banking system needs to become stronger, so as to avoid being the target of hostile takeovers from abroad. At the same time, it must also become more competitive, in order to support the necessary changes in the Greek economy: to finance the investments made by serious enterprises, assist households without fuelling unrestrained consumption, and make depositors feel confidence. In order to deal with the risk of certain businesses running out of liquidity and eventually collapsing, one or more 'bad banks' could be established, in the form of over-indebted Enterprise Banks (OEB). OEBs are separated from the banks' official portfolios, in order to help them get rid of 'toxic stock', but are being run by a syndicate of lender banks with no state participation. This way, instead of passing the cost of their own erroneous choices to the taxpayers, banks would be motivated to support private businesses and reap the benefits of the restructuring by including them again in their portfolios.

11.4. INVESTMENT RULES

It is worth recalling that in the aftermath of the financial crisis, whereas the most developed and connected banks of the Anglo-Saxon world did collapse, the banking system in countries such as France, Italy and Greece proved to be much more resilient. That was not due to any superior predictive power, but because the banks in these EU countries were more conservative and did not rush to join the financial exuberance. As strange as it may seem, they survived the crisis because they failed to seize the new toxic opportunities that had been presented to them as very promising ones.

Counting on this experience, the Greek banking system needs to move to the following directions:

i. Separating the banks' high-risk investment activities from the more conventional deposit-taking and lending operations. This is the only way to insulate depositors and borrowers from the risk of losses caused by reckless investments. Although this may sound sensible and true today, few opted for it before the crisis, since they enjoyed the windfall profits generated by the mass issuance of toxic assets.

ii. The most difficult thing, though, is not the imposition of supervision rules and systems, but the prevalence of financial products that are easy to choose and easy to understand, owing to their limited and acceptable risk content. If the financial engineering of complex products and derivatives is left unchecked, and their sale to the mass investing public goes unrestrained, then the pursuit of extra profits will once again become the norm and, sooner or later, the next crisis will approach.

iii. Setting new rules for investment firms. The tools provided for by corporate governance and corporate social responsibility regarding transparency, obligations and practices should apply not only to productive enterprises but also to hedge funds. After all, their largely unchecked practices are to a large extent responsible for causing the artificial rise of asset values, the collapse of which is now falling on the shoulders of many unsuspecting investors and countries.

11.5. A UNIFIED SOCIAL SECURITY SYSTEM

11.5.1. Widening Inequalities

The social security system in Greece is the source of widening inequality among citizens, both between employees of the same generation, and among the current and next generations. No wonder then that the system remains an area of severe political and social disagreement. In periods of reform those who protest are affected by the increase of retirement ages, the increase in replacement ratios, the re-examination of exceptional cases and the abolition of unfair provisions. This is a typical case where the privileged 'insiders' join forces to prevent any change in their privileged benefits.

But when no intervention is being made, those who worry are the underprivileged 'outsiders'. The reason is that, although they have properly paid their contributions and expect to get a pension without the facilitation of any notional years, it is highly probable that, by the time they retire, the reserves of their pension fund may have been depleted. This may happen either because they were used to finance the previous layer of pensioners or—even worse—have been transferred to the pension funds of 'insiders', who receive pensions without having paid their full contributions. This is exactly what happened in 2015 when the government, in lack of revenues sufficient to finance current expenditure, transferred the savings of social security funds to a central financial facility.

The alliance of privileged insiders includes the pension funds of PUCs and many banks, the professional funds (as those of engineers, lawyers, media employees etc.) that have been endowed with earmarked taxes and those who have secured normal pensions with limited contributions (Members of Parliament, mayors, employees of Parliament, artists, farmers etc.). They further include certain free-riders who have been included in various pension funds by purely political decisions (such as uninsured returnees from abroad, football players insured in the Seamen's Pension Fund and so forth). Those receiving low pensions or facing uncertainty about not getting one at all include all private sector employees, the actual seamen, most shop owners, the self-employed and small entrepreneurs.

There is also an in-between category of 'insider-outsiders' that includes public sector pensioners. Most of them have actually worked for the proper number of years, without notional years and transfers of rights. They are in between because, although they have properly paid their own contributions, their pensions are subsidized by the state budget more than private sector pensioners. Their pensions are also supplemented by numerous side benefits, dividends, subsidized low-cost mortgage loans and so forth.

Inter-generational inequality emerges from the distinction between those insured before and after 1993. The latter have to pay higher contributions and need to complete a longer working period before retiring. Owing to this inequality, younger workers are squeezed dry in order to finance the markedly higher pensions of current and imminent pensioners. As the situation will become more burdensome in the future, the inequality between generations acts as counter-incentive to stay and work in Greece. Combined with high unemployment, this drives many young people to emigrate and seriously harms the accumulation of human capital that is badly needed for the economic reconstruction of Greece.

11.5.2. Reform by Uniformity

Given all these inequalities, reforming the social security system in Greece will have an extensive effect on society in terms of efficiency, equity and equality before the law. This reform may gain such a momentum that it drives reforms in other sectors of the economy, as well as causing more general changes in social behaviour and values. This is due to the fact that the current social security system in Greece is a *multi-parameter* complex system, which tests the relations between:

a. salaried employees of the public and the private sectors
b. civil servants and PUC employees
c. political executives and business executives
d. previous, present and future generations
e. merchants and freelance professionals
f. professions vested with earmarked taxes and those without.

The Greek pension system can be described as an open 'pay-as-you-go' system. It is an uncertain and undefined model, in the sense that pensions are not determined on the basis of actual contributions being paid, but depend on the circumstances prevailing upon each person's retirement. This is exactly what fuels the insecurity of future pensioners, who are afraid that by the time they retire the huge deficits of their own pension fund, will cause their pensions to shrink.

The other extreme to the above framework is a 'fully-funded' system, which precludes social redistribution and is exclusively based on the future market return of individual contributions. The introduction of this model in Greece will create a host of new inequalities and lead to drastic reductions of many pensions especially during the transition period. Most likely, it will give rise to such a vehement resistance by insiders that all efforts to establish it will be frustrated.

A realistic compromise between the uncertainty of the *open* 'pay-as-you-go' system and the straightjackets of the 'fully-funded' system would be a *closed* 'pay-as-you-go' system. This functions with explicitly defined parameters concerning the co-financing of personal contributions through state participation. The proportion of subsidization may take into account the peculiarities of each trade specialization.

The unified pension fund may also introduce reward-penalty systems, along the *bonus-malus* schemes employed by insurance companies. The unified system may be structured on two pillars according to whether it includes wage earners and public sector employees or business owners and private sector professionals.

Pillar I. National Employees Insurance Fund

This includes all salaried employees, without any exception, irrespective of whether a person works as a boatman in a remote island, in the Greek embassy in Paris, or as a delivery boy in the local pizzeria. The same fund will include all ranks of civil servants and administration staff, from the heads of village councils to ministers, and from nurses to public enterprise managers.

Pillar II. National Business Insurance Fund

This includes all owners and/or practitioners of private business activities, merchants, freelance professionals, farmers, taxi drivers, truck owners, etc. All existing professional pension funds are merged into the new entity.

There will not be a third insurance fund. Given, though, that the aforementioned funds will only cover the 'closed-end cost' of their members' pensions and healthcare expenses, there is the risk that totally uninsured individuals, such as non-visa-granted immigrants, long-term unemployed, jobless small-rentiers, minors with uninsured parents or seniors with ungrateful children, may find themselves without any kind of coverage.

This way far outsider category can be covered by a third social agency, financed by the state budget, which offers healthcare and old-age benefits on the basis of purely social criteria, and without reciprocity rules.

How will it be possible to get all the currently extremely different categories of salaried employees and pensioners to register with the unified funds and be subject to uniform rules? Isn't this going to completely overturn 'entitlements', thus leading to formation of insider alliances that will prevent the changes?

Not necessarily. The unification of existing funds will be based on a carefully drafted transition plan and a road map of convergence towards the unified rules, without any loss in consummated 'entitlements'. In this case, the term 'entitlement' would denote the accrued part of preferential arrangements. The portion of the entitlement that is preserved will be easily calculated as the ratio of the years of employment up to that point to the total time remaining for the preferential arrangement to take full effect.

Suppose, for example, a person expects to receive a full pension after 25 years of work and has already worked for 15 years. When moved to the unified fund, this person will hold a fraction of 15/25 or 60% of the pension entitled to thus far. This amount will be supplemented by 20/35 of the new pension, in accordance with the subsequently uniform rules, provided that this person continues to work for 35 years. If, however, the person wishes to retire after just 25 years of work, as initially entitled to, then the additional amount will be equal to 10/35 or just 28% of the new pension. In this case, the total pension will amount to 88% of the initial arrangement.

11.5.3. Transition Rules

The implementation of the transition plan will obviously have to be based on the record of each social security account. This can be done through the introduction and issuance of a *Pension and Insurance Credit Account* (PICA) for *each* person insured. This will be in the form of a bank account and record the insurance contributions paid by the worker, and those paid by the state and the employer, as well as the state additions made to the paid contributions, in accordance with the parameters set for each fund and field of employment or trade.

The account is capitalized in regular intervals and the employees will be informed about the insurance credit accumulated up to that point, thus being aware of the pension capabilities they have established. This calculation gives them the option to select from a combination of retirement age and pensions that are all compatible with their accumulated savings. In case the employees are hired by an entity using different addition parameters, the pension capital is commensurately increased and the person insured will gain additional pension returns.

Thanks to the PICA, employees know exactly what has been paid every time, what the other two parties have supplemented and which pension they have established. This is also the easiest way of dealing with labour mobility among various sectors without any loss of insurance contributions, since all pension returns from each insurance period are added to the next. It is like transferring a deposit account into another bank. Today, the lack of insurance mobility across different pension funds makes it very difficult to switch employment or professional specialization, since this may entail losses in pension entitlements.

In conclusion, the political and financial advantages from the creation of two universal insurance funds are evident and extensive, including:

a. uninterrupted labour mobility without the loss of any social security contributions;
b. full transparency and disclosure of egregious pension inequalities;
c. easy calculation of the fiscal cost corresponding to each category;
d. freedom to choose retirement ages, as well as return to the labour market on the pensioners' discretion;
e. equality, partial for today's citizens and full for the future generations.

The social security unification will also terminate a preferential regime that is currently available for political personnel. Under very soft and limited conditions, elected officials may establish additional pension rights on top of the pension earned from their regular job they previously held. These extra pensions will be automatically abolished in the unified social security system. Pay differentials during their public service will simply augment social insurance contributions and the final pension, but without establishing claim on a separate one. This reform not only economizes on public expenditure but will have a profoundly symbolic meaning for equal treatment of citizens. Efficiency gains can be also realized as the political personnel will legislate

and supervise the regulations applicable to salaried employees in a more par-
simonious, careful and equitable manner.

***

A new framework clearly separating state and business activities was suggested to replace the corporatist and clientelistic relations that still characterize the Greek economy and are responsible for many of its deficiencies.
A major change, however, would be the establishment of a unified social
security system without the intra-generational inequalities and inter-generational injustices that continue to thrive in the present system. This reform can
bring about more fairness among different professions and generations and
will catalyze further reforms in Greek society at large. If, in contrast, Greece
remains in a reform limbo, impasses will multiply and the Grexit might
become more attractive for the least privileged. However, in no way is this
going to be more beneficial for them as the next chapter explains.

NOTES

1. US Exchange Act, Sections 13b, 2 A and B.
2. The Capital Market Code that was enacted in January 2004 transposed the
European Directive on Market Abuse, which corresponds to the US Sarbanes-Oxley
Act of 2002, into Greek law. The fines for market abuse-related offences had been
substantially increased, and were multiplied in the case of repeat offences.
3. The only exception concerns the pension funds that had been invested in
structured bonds, which had, nonetheless, been mainly purchased by state-controlled
banks.

Chapter 12

The Political Economy of Drachma

Lower Wages, More Inequalities

This chapter examines the consequences of a return of the drachma for wages and salaries, the banking system and the distribution of wealth, and concludes that a recession a lot more painful than the current adjustment would befall the economy. It also describes the capital flight since 2010 and shows how a drastic devaluation of the new currency would lead to a massive redistribution of wealth as the funds will repatriate at a much higher domestic value.

12.1. DEVALUE AND DIVIDE: THE REDISTRIBUTION MECHANISM

When a country devalues its currency, the goods it produces automatically become cheaper in terms of international prices. As a result, exports may rise, while imported goods become more expensive in terms of domestic prices, and demand for them is likely to decrease. If these things do actually occur, then the trade deficit improves and the country is unburdened from the foreign borrowing required to finance it. In reality, though, developments are rarely so simple. The devaluation triggers a series of processes that seriously mitigate, or may even negate, the expected outcome for reasons described below.

12.1.1. Wage Earners and Businesses

First of all, domestic production costs will be driven up by the rise in prices of imported intermediate goods, and, as a result, the international price of the final product will be reduced by only a fraction of devaluation. Domestic inflation will increase for the same reason, and wage earners will demand pay rises, in order to make up for the loss of purchasing power they automatically suffer. If they are successful, the labour cost of production will rise and, combined with the increase in the cost of imported goods, wipe out any benefit from devaluation.

The only way to avert such an outcome is to impose discipline on workers' demands, prohibiting them from claiming pay rises and thus leading to a reduction of real wages. This is why devaluations always go hand in hand with prolonged wage freezes, aimed at reducing labour costs and thus boosting the profitability of firms. In Greece, the devaluation of the drachma in 1983 led to the abolition of automatic inflation-linked wage adjustment, while the devaluation of 1985 was combined with the legal prohibition of all kinds of wage increases, even in the private sector. Devaluations improve labour cost competitiveness only when wage discipline is simultaneously imposed, and it is obvious that in real terms this constitutes a mechanism for redistributing income from workers to the business sector. This is hardly an option that can be uncritically endorsed by Left-wing supporters of Grexit.

A similar rationale regarding the need to reduce labour costs in order to improve competitiveness of Greek products has been adopted by the Memorandum. Given that currency devaluation—through a reduction in the value of the euro solely for Greece—is not possible, the so-called 'internal devaluation' was devised. In this case, the reduction in real wages is not achieved through inflation but by an outright reduction of nominal wages. The outcome is the same, and its realization requires a similar mechanism for imposing discipline on pay-rise demands; in 2011, this was achieved through the suspension, or complete suppression, of collective bargaining in both the public and private sectors.

However, even a combination of external or internal devaluation and wage discipline cannot guarantee a structural improvement of trade deficits if exports are characterized by low penetration in global markets and/or imports are inelastic due to the lack of local substitutes. These conditions are determined by more profound features of the economy that cannot easily change at short notice, and this is why sometimes devaluations have only meagre results. For example, the 1983 and 1985 devaluations led to only temporary increases in exports. The internal devaluation of 2011 had the same result. As already discussed in chapter 4, private sector wages were reduced by 22%, but exports improved only marginally in 2012 and remained stagnant in 2013, demonstrating how immaterial and temporary the improvement of competitiveness is that results from driving down labour costs.[1]

Imports seem to have been more influenced by the internal devaluation, albeit their reduction is not largely attributable to encouraging their substitution by domestically produced goods, but mainly to the drop in total demand caused by the reduction of wages. The wage cut produces another gap as business incomes improve for the firm owners but not for their workers. Demand for imports by the former is not affected, and this magnifies the uneven distribution of consumption goods between rich and poor households.

12.1.2. Depositors and Borrowers

Devaluation brings about sea changes in the relative value of wealth. A business, whose exports and profits grow as a result of devaluation, sees its value increase as compared to the income it distributes to its workers. This usually leads to the rapid growth of capital markets and the equally rapid deterioration of the position of wage-dependent households. After Argentina devalued its currency, the peso had lost three-quarters of its value against the dollar by 2008. However, the value of the MERVAL index of the Buenos Aires Stock Exchange increased by a factor of 13. Property values also increase in relation to domestic incomes and, as a result, poor households find it more difficult to get a house of their own.

The external devaluation does not affect the nominal amount of deposits in local currency, but their real value decreases nonetheless, because the goods and services this money can buy become more costly. In the case of a currency replacement, things are more complicated, because changes in wealth values are determined by the conversion rate that will be applied to bank deposits and loan agreements. Assuming that loans and deposits in Greece are converted on the basis of the exchange rate that applied upon entry to the single currency, that is, 341 drachmas per euro, bank deposits will suffer a huge decline in real terms, since the exchange rate of the new currency will be steeply devalued and will likely deteriorate a lot further afterwards.

In the case of a standard (external) devaluation, bank deposits in local currency automatically suffer a 'haircut' in terms of internal purchasing power. Given that the value of loans is similarly reduced in real terms, this sets in motion a mechanism that redistributes wealth from creditors to debtors. Once again, this process leads to the same outcomes with certain aspects of the adjustment programmes implemented in the Eurozone. For example, a cut in deposits was implemented in the case of Cyprus in 2013. Since the currency could not be devalued through a change in the exchange rate, an internal 'haircut' of deposits was devised. In such a case, the effects of a Grexit would look ominously similar to those policies the drachma supporters today rush to denounce.

12.2. THE GREXIT PUT IN PRACTICE

Let's see now in more detail, what could happen if the Grexit scenario were realized, either as a deliberate choice of some Greek government, or because

Greece was forced to leave through a combination of further pressures and new impasses. As in other currency collapses, the first step is sovereign default, which would be triggered at a certain point by the state's refusal or inability to repay its debt. Overseas houses would immediately put this down as a credit event, and the new situation would be swiftly communicated to creditors all over the world, irrespective of the maturity of the Greek sovereign bonds they hold. Realizing that the country's inability to repay its loans may possibly concern everyone, the lenders would respond by cutting off its access to credit, no matter if it is supplied by market investors or the Troika institutions. In the next phase, the state would not have enough money to cover its operating requirements and would resort to a partial suspension of salaries and pensions. Subsequently, it would be forced to discontinue the provision of vital services in many sectors, due to the interruption of supply with goods that can either be purchased only by cash on delivery, or have to be imported.

Greece would find itself desperately seeking credit, but, still being a member of the Eurozone and unable to print its own money, it would turn to the ECB and possibly get a small and brief liquidity lifeline. However, this will eventually cease, as the ECB will sustain losses from the collapse of Greek government bonds in the secondary market and would have to minimize its exposure. Although it would be possible to use the 'big bazooka' of quantitative easing with unlimited OMTs, the ECB would probably refuse to do so in case it sees that exit is inevitable. [2]

And so we would enter the third phase, when ECB's withdrawal would be denounced as an 'act of treason' and some quarters would recommend a heroic exit from the repressive fortress of Europe. Under such stifling conditions, they would make the desperate and unpaid parts of the population welcome this as redemption. The government would probably sell this as 'uncompromising national strategy', which would give Greece its own currency back, without any EU strings attached. In fact it will be intact, since the country would have ceased paying its foreign lenders. And this would immediately lead to a freefall, with the following consequences:

12.2.1. Credit Asphyxiation

First and foremost, no lender will ever forget Greece. Creditor states would immediately seek recourse against Greece in European and international courts, claiming full compensation from the Greek state and the confiscation of the country's available assets.

The most recent relevant example is that of Argentina, where public debt was unilaterally written off. Creditors then appealed to US courts, which, after many years, decided in their favour.[3] Still, Argentina defied pressures, having on its side not only its citizens, but also a substantial part of the international public, which was enraged with the private creditors' greediness against a struggling nation. But when the country entered a repayment crisis in the beginning of 2014, she lost a large part of its foreign exchange reserves seeking financing from abroad, and all the doors were found to be closed. At that point, the government of Argentina offered to compensate the lenders it had written off, by proposing a compromise.

But by that time the balance of power had shifted: sensing the dire situation the government had gotten into, the lenders that had previously sought legal recourse rejected the proposal, causing the pressures on the currency to intensify. In just a few days the peso was again devalued and automatically the value of the country's foreign debt was multiplied, making repayment even more difficult. In an effort to defend the currency, the government put a ban on foreign exchange exports and imposed a heavy tax on imports, even on travels abroad. The result was, of course, predictable, as in the case of 1932 Greece: panic soared, the exchange rate in the black market multiplied and Argentina faced the possibility of a new collapse.

If Greece opted for a unilateral debt write-off, the reactions would be somewhat different: admittedly, such an action would be supported by a part of the Greek society that is looking forward to its liberation from the 'debts to the foreigners', but it would be very difficult to find supporters among the European public. The reason is that this time the holders of Greek debt are mainly the other member states of the Eurozone and, therefore, any legal action against Greece would not take the convenient guise of greedy speculators versus a bankrupt country, but that of state versus state.

The fact that some of the countries that have lent money to Greece have lower per capita incomes—as, for example, Slovakia, Slovenia and Portugal—would make such legal action take the opposite character: poor nations versus a more well-off country that swindled them. Greece's exclusion from international markets would make the—already scarce—investors even more reluctant, while the financial panic within the country would lead to a persistent lack of liquidity. In order to compensate for their losses, the poorer countries might try to block any financial assistance to Greece from the EU's structural funds, automatically depriving the country of growth-related finance. This would ignite new fronts of conflict with Community authorities and fuel the dynamics of complete disengagement from the European Union.[4] The cost for the nation would be immeasurable and chronic.

It is interesting to compare the consequences of a Grexit with those of a *Nexit*, that is, the Netherlands' exit from the euro and the European Union. A recent study, commissioned by the Netherlands' far-right Party for Freedom

(*Partij voor de Vrijheid*, PvV), showed that the greatest gains for the Dutch economy will stem from the fact that the country will stop paying contributions to the EU.[5] Since Greece is a net recipient of European funds, the reasonable conclusion is that it would suffer a major decline in living standards, even if all other things worked in its favour—something that will not happen anyway, as discussed below.

12.2.2. Speculation

A currency replacement is fundamentally different from the case of a currency leaving a fixed exchange rate system and moving to a new regime, albeit keeping the same physical form of coins and notes. In the latter case, it suffices to make an announcement one Friday evening, after the markets close, and on Monday morning trading may resume under the new exchange rate. In contrast, a currency replacement is a complex process, even when the situation is perfectly normal and there is no uncertainty at all among the trading partners. The preparation and testing for the introduction of the euro—which was eagerly expected by all countries—lasted for many months, in order to solve a host of problems related to price conversions and the adequate cash supply of ATMs.

Assuming a transition to a new currency in Greece, the situation would be close to panic. No matter how the government of the day would try to expedite the transition, the technical procedure for the design and issuance of a new currency would require a few months, during which many accidents could occur.

To begin with, the government would have to decide whether to first announce the transition to the new currency and then initiate the preparations for its issuance, or first complete the preparations in secrecy and then decide on a Grexit. In the former case, the euro would immediately vanish from the market, since hoarding would subsequently increase its value. As preparations start, liquidity will disappear and most transactions would be either cancelled or performed by barter. Given that—economically speaking—a month is a very long period of time, the events that may occur would add to uncertainty, exacerbating the feeling of insecurity.

In case preparations are held in secrecy, insiders would indulge in a frenetic speculation, which would soon be noticed and more people would follow suit. Even if, for reasons of confidentiality, printing the new currency was assigned to a foreign state, the country would be vulnerable to speculative attacks and manoeuvring. The introduction of the new currency would not only be accompanied by a steep devaluation, but would also give rise to fears of an impending doom.

12.2.3. Prolonged Currency Volatility

Drachma evangelists foster the impression that, should Greece leave the euro, it would return to the situation that prevailed just before 2000, when the currency was stable and, what is more, was 'ours'. But there will be no such return to the drachma of the year 2000; just the creation of a different currency with a different value, and perhaps with a different name. For convenience, let this be called the New Drachma.

After the new currency is designed, the government should have to decide on its initial exchange rate, as well as on the system used for managing it with every change in external or competitiveness conditions. Today, the official reference exchange rate is 341 drachmas per euro; this rate is considered by many analysts to be non-competitive and is one of the main arguments in favour of a Grexit. Therefore, it is almost certain that there will be an initial devaluation of at least 50%, in order to overcompensate for the competitiveness differential with the other Eurozone countries and, in particular, with Germany and leave some room for future gains. Thus, the devalued currency would be launched at a rate of almost 500 New Drachma/€. The next decision of the government will be on whether the new currency should be left to freely float in the foreign exchange market or will be pegged to a stable currency—for example, the US dollar or, again, the euro. The latter option would seem schizophrenic. After rejecting it as the common currency, yet pegging the new one to the euro might be the most likely option as Greece's main partner would still be the European economies.

Let's begin with the currency peg: Given that the New Drachma will be viewed, at least initially, as an unstable currency, maintaining the fixed exchange rate would require an increase in interest rates at levels much higher than European or American ones. This will soon sink the economy into further recession and force the government to make a new devaluation. If the pressure is sustained, the authorities will impose severe restrictions on capital movements, obstructing international trade and giving rise to phenomena of foreign exchange hoarding and capital flight that were frequent in the 1970s and 1980s. This way, bearish expectations will become permanent, putting relentless pressure on the currency.

Since the main reason invoked by the authorities for exiting the euro would be the Greek economy's recession, many people will expect, or push for, greater devaluations, thus leading to a transitional period of instability that will be difficult to be dealt with under the controlled exchange rate regime discussed above. Thus, the New Drachma will very likely be placed under a free float regime for some time, until markets are persuaded about the sustainability of the exchange rate that will finally prevail. This is when the well-known phenomenon of 'exchange rate overshooting' will occur and the new currency will immediately undergo another great devaluation, possibly exceeding the initial one. Eventually, the New Drachma will become much cheaper, with its exchange rate even falling to 750 per euro or more.

When the New Drachma currency becomes that cheap, some of the expatriated capital will start flowing back into Greece in order to acquire assets at fire-sale prices, and the exchange rate will show some improvement. No one can predict where it will finally settle. It is reasonable to assume that instability will become endemic, since all the above will occur in conjunction with the overall international currency realignments caused by Greece's exit.

The available historical examples are rather frightening: In the aftermath of the 1932 collapse, the drachma was initially devalued by 85% against the US dollar, but by the end of that year its value had tumbled by 140%. It took several years to recover and was only by the end of the 1930s that it returned to an exchange rate depreciated by 83% against the dollar[6].

The outcome of the introduction of a new currency immediately after Greece's liberation from the Axis Occupation was much worse. In 1944, the exchange rate against the dollar stood at 149 drachmas; in 1945 it rose to 500; and in 1949 it reached 15,000 drachmas per US dollar, because each new currency change proved to be non-credible and non-sustainable. When the New Drachma was introduced at a fixed exchange rate against the British gold sovereign, all cash reserves and deposits were converted to sovereigns and hoarded away, since nobody believed that the exchange rate could be sustained at that level. The authorities were once again forced to replace the currency and introduce the third modern Drachma, which was devalued again in 1953 before being pegged to the US dollar—the only reason it remained stable for the following twenty years.[7]

12.2.4. Inflation and Wages

The successive devaluations will cause rampant inflation, perhaps as high as 50%. In this sense, it will be more reminiscent not of the 1990s, the period for which all Grexit proposals are so nostalgic of, but the hyperinflation years immediately after the Axis Occupation as mentioned above.

The purchasing power of wages would be immediately reduced by almost 50%, one-to-one as the rise in inflation. Then it would be further eroded by chronic inflation. Not everybody is hit in the same way though. Workers in export companies might somewhat mitigate their losses thanks to increased production and sales bonuses. Public sector salaries will be forced down by devaluation and inflation. However, employees in certain privileged public sector organizations and corporations may still find ways to be compensated through the implementation of special payroll systems, and will not suffer as much as ordinary civil servants.

12.3. THE BANKING QUAKE

12.3.1. Debtors and Creditors

Greek banks will be dealt a heavy blow as a result of the implicit 'haircut' on their Greek sovereign bond holdings, without having the option of being recapitalized through the Eurozone anymore. In addition, the ECB will not anymore be providing them with liquidity, since Greece will not be a member of the Eurosystem. At the same time, they will be besieged by depositors demanding to withdraw their savings in euros because those who entrusted the banks with their money will insist that this is how they should stay. The banks would agree on such an arrangement only if the loans they have extended in euros were repaid in this currency; however, this is not economically feasible, for two reasons: first, because businesses will be operating under the new currency and all their obligations will be denominated in it. If their loans continued to be denominated in euros, this would lead to a revaluation of their debt, forcing them to cease operating. Second, families with house loans will be paid their wages in new drachmas and, of course, will not be able to survive if their mortgage continues to be denominated in euros, because it will be automatically increased by devaluation.

In order to prevent the huge appreciation of private debts, the government will inevitably resort to the devaluation of deposits. Their conversion to drachmas at the exchange rate of the first day means that their value will subsequently be further eroded by the continuous depreciation of the currency. This procedure represents the second redistribution mechanism that the currency change will set in motion: from depositors to debtors. The losers will include those households that were prudently saving for years, while those that borrowed frequently and prodigally will be the winners. The losers will also include those businesses that were profitable and regularly saved their profits in order to make new investments, while winners will include struggling businesses that were unable to meet their debt obligations. The resulting situation will be tantamount to a 'debtor's paradise' and a 'creditor's hell', although it will probably be given the political disguise of another 'people's battle' against the banking system.

In practice, this will amount to a *de facto* seizure of deposits, as was the case in Argentina in 2002, which led to a sudden redistribution of wealth and widespread social unrest. In Greece, similar phenomena occurred in 1923, when the authorities forced the citizens to cut the banknotes in two halves and give one to the state; a little later with the 1932 devaluation; and when hyperinflation erased debts and wiped out savings after the Axis Occupation. According to an analyst of the time:[8]

the blow that was inflicted on the Greek economy was immense and unprecedented. Entire fortunes, savings and deposits of poor families, small tradesmen, employees . . . which were their only assets, their only support . . . all went up in smoke, vanished from one moment to the other.

But then there was a critical difference: the situation following the Axis Occupation was so tragic on every stretch of life that such grievances were soon overshadowed by the impending civil war, which led to a new national calamity. This is why all devaluation-related events were engraved on the collective memory as second-order disasters, since what ultimately mattered was physical survival. Under today's conditions, the onset of economic disaster is not likely to be overshadowed by other perils, despite possible provocations to fuel a climate of conflict that would disguise an exit from the euro as a national 'liberation'. The financial blow that will be inflicted on households and business's savings will be felt for many years and pose a permanent impediment to reconstruction efforts.

Gains will also be realized by property owners, who will automatically adjust prices upwards in order to compensate for their losses in international valuation terms. Social security funds will face a new crisis, on top of the 2012 haircut through which their reserves have been already wiped out. With lower real wages and national insurance contributions, it will not be possible to save enough and replace the loss in the purchasing power of pensions. Thus, the abandonment of the euro will lead to a dramatic increase of inequality and poverty.

12.3.2. Business and Wealth

Many small and medium-sized enterprises will survive by squeezing their profits, thus making it easier to export their products. Being wary, though, of a new devaluation, they will be probably keeping their profits abroad, as they used to do in the past, instead of investing them in Greece. Firms that use imported materials will be forced to raise their prices, thus setting off an inflationary spiral and further shrinking domestic demand.

After the introduction of the New Drachma, Greek firms will be facing increased costs of trading with other European countries, because they will be engaging in cross-currency transactions and have to take insurance against currency risk. The loss of access to European structural funds means that they will be deprived of the means necessary for promoting innovation and training, and will be put at a disadvantage vis-à-vis European competitors. Eventually, any gain from the reduction of labour costs will end up being inferior to the direct or indirect costs that Greek firms are going to incur.

12.3.3. The Unemployed

This is currently the toughest problem, because unemployment has reached exorbitant levels and anything that could possibly reduce it seems like a nice idea. It is indeed true that a drastic devaluation would reduce unemployment, albeit the extent and speed of this improvement is questionable. For example, after the 1932 devaluation, unemployment continued to rise for quite a few years. It remained completely unaffected by the 1983 devaluation, and was only temporarily improved as a result of the 1985 devaluation. In any case, though, any improvement will be simply due to the dramatic drop in real wages.

In other words, what will actually reduce unemployment is not the adoption of a national currency *per se*, but the fact that the new currency will be used as a mechanism for hiring the jobless at a much lower wage. In fact, this is exactly the objective of Memorandum. Its policies precisely aim at increasing employment through the internal devaluation of wages and the deregulation of the labour market.

Treating the two policy options as equivalent may sound like sacrilege to those that simultaneously present themselves as anti-Memorandum protesters and anti-euro hardliners. The difference between the Memorandum and the New Drachma is, however, immaterial, since the end result in both cases will be the reduction in real wages. Only the method is different: in the case of an external devaluation, the adjustment is immediate and carried out by a decision of the Bank of Greece, whereas an internal devaluation requires many different sets of legislation, which lead to time-consuming procedures until they are finalized. This gives rise to a paradox of political inconsistency: those in favour of dealing with unemployment by reducing real wages should, logically, also be zealously supporting the Memorandum's wage-reducing policies, though they appear otherwise. Ideological prejudice notwithstanding this is a common ground of the seemingly opposing policies.

The real issue is whether society chooses to deal with mass unemployment by squeezing real wages. Several studies have shown that labour costs have a limited effect on the competitiveness of the Greek economy and this is why the internal devaluation has hardly led so far to an increase in exports or employment. So, it is highly possible that even the external devaluation of the new currency may not lead to a substantial rise in employment. Society, will at the end, have lost a strong and reliable currency for a nebulous or perhaps no real benefit.

12.3.4. Turbulence in the Eurozone

Despite the temporary complications for their markets and banking sectors, Greece's exit from the Eurozone will be welcomed with great relief by the remaining countries. Some parties will try to gain political capital by presenting it to their continually protesting public as atonement for the assistance offered to a bankrupt state, while others may seize the opportunity to introduce austerity policies so as to avoid 'becoming Greece'. At the same time, the unity of the euro will be severely shaken, as the exit game will immediately commence for Portugal, Italy and Spain.[9] Whatever remains of the euro will be depreciated, and its use as a reserve currency will be decreased worldwide.

Perhaps one may assume that this would be of no interest to Greece, since it will be out of the euro, but this is wrong. Even if the destabilization of the euro will improbably lead to the demise of the Eurozone and the return of national currencies, any gains realized by Greek exports to European countries will disappear. Every individual nation will have to resort to beggar-thy-neighbour devaluations, dragging each other to even deeper recession.

12.4. NEW CURRENCY AND NEW RICHES

When the value of a currency collapses, the corporate assets that are still denominated in the devalued currency attract great interest from the holders of non-depreciated capital—simply because the latter can now buy much more.

Following the devaluation of the peso, Argentina suddenly became a speculator's El Dorado: after having lost two-thirds of its value, the economy started—as is the case following every major disaster—to recover and the much-needed investments immediately found their backers. The share of investment expenditure in Argentina started to increase rapidly, reversing the downturn that preceded the crisis, as illustrated in chapter 8 in more detail. From a mere US dollar 11 billion spending in 2001, investment expenditure gradually[10] rose to USD 113 billion by 2012, an increase of more than USD 100 billion. Coincidentally, the increase is roughly equal to the amount of capital that previously had fled the country!

Flight capital was being repatriated *en masse*, acquiring property and business assets for peanuts. At the same time, bank deposits of small households were blocked, because the authorities wanted to prevent a bank run by panic-stricken citizens who saw their wealth, not only vanish in thin air, but also change hands and come to the possession of the few that had rushed to speculate. This is how Naomi Klein—a fervent supporter of third world countries against globalization—describes the situation that prevailed in 2003:[11]

> for many of Argentina's richest families and businesses, the banking fiasco and devaluation . . . actually made them richer than they were before: they now pay their employees, their expenses and their debts in devalued pesos, but—thanks to the banks—their savings are safely stored outside the country in US dollars. It's a highly profitable arrangement.

If Greece left the euro, it would face the same conditions of currency collapse that will turn the opportunistic return of flight capital into an extremely profitable venture. Many assets and business will change hands in an unprecedented scale, resembling the ascent of oligarchs in the post-communist societies of Eastern European countries. Rather than being the wind of liberation from the 'euro prison' that the single currency's opponents keep trumpeting about, the Grexit process will likely lead to the emergence and domination of a new oligarchy.

12.5. GEOPOLITICAL DISARRAY

Greece's exit from the euro will distort all coordinates of current geopolitical reference and will drive the country into unchartered waters. Since it will most probably be the result of a disorderly capital flight, the new landscape will not enable any strategic redesign, even towards controversial directions. The most likely outcome will be Greece's isolation, not only from the European Union but also from any extra-European options.

For example, any redesign of Greece's strategic presence outside Europe that will seek to capitalize on the current transitional situation in the countries of North Africa and the Middle East, will probably be futile. No country that aspires to economic progress and stability would like to be connected with a country that has just been downgraded on both aspects. Thus, the divorce from the euro will not represent an opportunity to play a different and possibly upgraded regional role, but one more step towards economic uncertainty and geopolitical marginalization.

***

The clear conclusion from the above analysis is that the shortcomings and ill-intended consequences of a Grexit would by far outweigh the slim benefits of a currency replacement. Wage earners would see their purchasing power fall a lot further than the levels enforced by the Memorandum, while new inequalities are going to emerge as repatriated capital buys out national property at fire-sale prices.

NOTES

1. Non-oil exports in 2012 were €14594.3, €14593.6 and €15458.7 million in 2012, 2013 and 2014, respectively. Data from http://www.bankofgreece.gr/Bog Ekdoseis/sdos201501-02.pdf. Table VI.7.

2. OMTs: Outright Market Transactions. The governor of the ECB has stated that he will do 'whatever it takes' to respond to speculative attacks.

3. These appeals are undertaken by specialized law firms that receive a percentage of the compensation. In Argentina, they are known as 'mosquitoes' or 'horseflies', for obvious reasons.

4. Pisani-Ferry, in his book '*Le réveil des démons*' (The awakening of the demons), claims that this process will be automatic, because 'no country can leave the euro and stay in the Union', (p. 155 of the Greek edition).

5. For the study, consult Chaloner J., A. Evans and M. Pragnell (2014).

6. The exchange rate stood at 77 drachmas/USD in March 1932; 146 GRD/USD in May 1932, just after the crisis; 185 GRD/USD in December 1932; and 141 GRD/USD in December 1939. Data: Bank of Greece.

7. Data from the Bank of Greece: (1947), *Governor's Report for the years 1941–46* (in Greek), (1978), *The first fifty years* (in Greek), Table 34, p. 255.

8. G. Maimoukas, 1945, *Forty five days of economic policy* (in Greek), p. 86.

9. This is what N. Rubini wrote in the *Financial Times* on 6/14/2011, arguing that other countries will be hit by Greece's devaluation and will follow its exit.

10. Calculations based on IMF data on investment and GDP, WEO Database.

11. N. Klein, "Out of the ordinary", *The Guardian*, 25/1/2003.

Epilogue

After the Left's Victory in Greece

COUNTDOWN

In 2014, two opposite signs appeared in the political scene of Greece. On the one hand, there had been a number of fiscal achievements on which the Greek government, as well as many European officials, had tried to capitalize some political gains. As explained in the Introduction, Greek deficits were put under control, and some positive—though tiny—growth was finally recorded after six consecutive years of contraction. Taking stock of these developments, the Greek government rushed to organize a 'success story' campaign, on its way to the European elections in May 2014, based on three elements:

Distributing: To cement support from traditional constituencies and thus contain their sway to the Left, the conservative party decided to use part of the primary surplus to finance handouts to the armed forces and the police. Similarly, the socialist partner of the coalition demanded that another part should go to poor pensioners so that they do not shift their vote to the marching Left. In practice, however, this small fiscal laxity proved to be too little too late to change the political dynamics, as already has been demonstrated in Table 1.1.

Issuing: Imitating the actions of the Irish and Portuguese authorities that had just returned to normal borrowing practices, the Greek government decided to tap markets with a limited bond auction after four years in the wilderness. Though the move was hailed by European leaders as showing that, after all, their own taxpayers' money did have an effect, most market analysts remained unimpressed. A plan for a second auction in autumn 2014 was abandoned.

Rescheduling: The fiasco with the multipliers and the continuation of recession and high unemployment had helped several European and international authorities to realize that the austerity programme was causing possibly irreparable damage to the Greek economy. This created a rare opportunity for the Greek government to put a claim on a new debt rescheduling and organize a coordinated exit from the Memorandum surveillance. There were sympathetic voices from all three Troika institutions and there was wide hope that a few remaining reform obligations would be easily accomplished.

But as happens with all superficial strategies, the Greek success story was derailed by relatively small mistakes and adversities. Had the strategy been robust and convincing, such details could possibly be arranged in the process. At that time, however, the government was facing two problems, one domestic and one from abroad, that eventually turned out to be too difficult to overcome.

The domestic flaw was the enactment of a new unified real-estate tax designed to replace the discredited special property levy imposed in 2011. The new tax was—once again—ill-prepared, laden with mistakes and untested with a selection of actual cases. Though for most proprietors the new tax was meant not to exceed the levy, there were many miscalculated cases that won widespread publicity. A wave of protest from small owners undercut the traditional voting base of the coalition parties and led to distinctive defeat in the European elections in May 2009. The Radical Left party came out on top signalling the potential to win a general election as well, while at the same time the extreme right reached nearly 10% of the vote, despite the fact that its leadership had been jailed on conspiracy charges and violent acts.

This was followed by a second mishap: in the summer of 2014, the government tried to steer the boat by unilaterally declaring that the process of disentanglement from the Troika had begun. Symbolism ran so high, that meetings were scheduled to take place in non-official venues in Paris, so as to signal that the situation was relaxed and the termination of the Memorandum was imminent. None of the meetings was successful and a new impasse emerged in autumn 2014. It was apparent that European authorities were not convinced that the adjustment has been completed, and the Troika demanded further cuts and refused to unconditionally grant a period of precautionary credit line as a backup to ending the programme.

The war of nerves culminated in December 2014 and the coalition government decided to 'bet the farm' by calling for an early presidential election. By this move, the government hoped to win an easy victory that would automatically give it a leeway of nearly two more years in power. It would also provide all the necessary time needed to convince European authorities that it had kept control of political developments, thus the bailout exit could be successfully negotiated.

Calculations proved to be erroneous, the presidential candidate did not attract the qualified majority and general elections were unavoidably set at the end of January 2015. The coalition parties were defeated, the Radical Left party, Syriza, came to power and the austerity programme collapsed.

GAME STRATAGEMS

The ground for a more flexible approach to the Greek crisis was already set before the elections when 18 prominent economists—including Nobel Laureates Joseph Stiglitz and Chris Pissarides—published an appeal in the *Financial Times* declaring 'that the whole of Europe will benefit from Greece being given the chance of a fresh start', including debt relief and less austerity.[1] In the aftermath of the 2015 elections and the sweeping domination of Syriza, international and European opinion was surprised to discover how vastly the austerity programme had failed to get Greece out of the crisis. As a response, a more sympathetic attitude spread across Europe that serious amendments were needed to fight recession and curb unemployment.

Post-elections, the collapse of mainstream political parties led many to support the new government and to give it a chance to rebuild the country. European and world political leaders (including US President Barack Obama), renowned academics and top international media expressed their support to Greece and pledged to contribute to search for a solution that gives Greece some breathing space and keeps it in the Eurozone. An early approach between the new government and European authorities led to a common statement announced on 20 February 2015, and there was optimism that an agreement would soon follow. But then the process was once more stalled by ill-planned tactics and histrionics.

The reason was that the European authorities, in exchange for disbursing new funds to Greece for repaying maturing obligations to the bailout partners, were demanding a list of fiscal measures and reforms so that the programme remains on track. Their fear was that the enactment of new expansionary policies could derail the programme and frustrate public opinion and taxpayers in the lender countries.

The new government was adamant about not adopting any recessionary measure and soon a new impasse emerged between the two sides: in a media overdose, Greek officials targeted their criticism mainly against European institutions, and Germany more specifically. German and EU officials reiterated the criticism and warned Greece that failure to meet her obligations may spark off a credit event and eventually jeopardize Greece's place in the Eurozone. Occasionally, the situation became very confrontational, with the Greek government warning about the contagious effects of such an eventuality.

International media adopted a game-theoretic framework in describing the new developments, thus giving an academic flair to the suffocation of the Greek economy that was becoming more evident by the day. Seeing the forthcoming impasse, analysts branded the situation as a 'game of chicken' whereas one party eventually succumbs so a major catastrophe is avoided. In the beginning, most of the commentators were suggesting that Germany plays the 'chicken' in recognition of the vastly unworkable austerity policies that its government had imposed upon Greece. Joseph Stiglitz pointedly declared that 'Greece made a few mistakes . . . but Europe made even bigger mistakes. The medicine they gave was poisonous. It led the debt to grow up and the economy to go down'. Therefore, it was clear who has to back off in the negotiations since 'Greece [is] not the problem, Germany is'.[2]

Even the US government strongly advised all sides to find a common ground and not risk any further uncertainty at a time when Europe was facing Russia's intransigence over Ukraine and a clear threat from the advancing *jihadists* in the Middle East. But against all the good omens, pro-Greek euphoria did not last for long. The Greek government was soon revealed to have no concrete policy plan to take up the challenge and kick-start the economy if left without Eurozone support. As the European institutions were insisting on some conditionality programme, analysts started pointing to the cooperative character of the game, whereas both sides can benefit by consensually reaching an agreement. The chances of such an outcome were enhanced after the summit in March 2015 between the German chancellor and the Greek PM.

Still, a number of foreign policy initiatives and domestic developments shifted the government's attention away from settling with the Eurozone. The government initiated a series of high-level contacts with China and Russia, which were domestically presented as building alternatives against potential isolation from EU. However, these proved to be very thin tactics: China was in absolutely no mood to play against the EU, while Russia carefully avoided any possible financial commitment towards indebted Greece. The only remaining non-EU potential supporter was the United States but that was alienated too by a sudden decision of the Greek government to soften imprisonment terms for convicted terrorists.

Time was running out and Greece was losing the sympathy capital that had initially accumulated. The next move was bluffing: there was widespread belief that the government in Athens was deliberately delaying the announcement of a reform list, so that funds would not be disbursed in time and repayment to the creditor organizations would be stalled *de facto*. In this case, the organization has the discretion to delay the declaration of a credit event for a few days, so that Greece is not immediately considered as officially defaulting. Of course, markets would miss no time to react and, in the ensuing speculation of an imminent Grexit, the euro would plunge, forcing creditors to revise their attitude towards Greece.

A possible opportunity for exercising the move was in the beginning of April 2015, when a repayment of €460 million was due to the IMF. The amount due was relatively small so as not to be considered as the ultimate threat to the credit system but just enough to probe the markets in rehearsing the consequences of a major event. A picket line was organized in central Athens urging the government to refuse paying the Fund and default on debt obligations altogether.[3] The response by the IMF left no room for such calculations: the government was readily summoned to the Washington headquarters and declared that '. . . Greece intended to meet all obligations to all its creditors, *ad infinitum*'.[4]

Party hardliners attempted to repeat the threat against European creditors but soon realized that it could mean setting off an uncontrollable series of events. International and European sympathy has mostly waned and changed to exasperation with everybody now asking Greece to find a workable solution with the bailout partners. The change of climate was acidly summarized by a Eurogroup official stating that '[t]his game of chicken is turning into Angry Birds'.[5]

In May 2015 and amid mounting financial difficulties and the continuing drain of deposits from Greek banks, a new list of reforms was proposed and an interim agreement was at last reached, giving some breathing space for the government. However, the major challenge has been set for July 2015 when a substantial repayment should be honoured by Greece. As it is obvious that such obligations can only be met by sizeable new disbursements, an agreement has to be struck including more far-reaching policies. To achieve this and to negotiate an orderly exit from the bailout programme, the Greek government has to discipline its internal hardliners and persuade its coalition nationalists.

Perhaps new elections or a referendum may be proposed to provide legitimacy to the government for U-turning from its pre-electoral commitments. Though it is far from given that such a process can resolve the existing political difficulties, it is certain that it would definitely usher in a new period of speculation, capital flight and stagnation. For as long as the issue is not decisively dealt with by a comprehensive agreement between the creditor institutions and Greece, the risk of Grexit and the ensuing chaos will continue to loom.

MISSING STRATEGY

Along the lines described in Part IV of this book, the government could forge a new negotiation strategy including the following steps:

a. Repay the relatively small IMF instalments due in 2015, thus keeping the Fund away from the negotiation table and concentrate on the issues related to the ECB and the Eurogroup. Such a move would allow the government to bypass the Fund—at least for a while—and focus on the European institutions which have more complex decision-making processes but at the same time are more flexible in taking into account political and social considerations.

b. Endorse a national plan of reforms and fiscal adjustment which is distinctly outside the mandate of the Memorandum. Thus, the government could appeal on the domestic public opinion that the policy framework is not any more a dictation from abroad, but the starting point for truly ending the intervention period and launching a new period of growth.

The plan would set specific deficit targets, privatizations, new investment and job creation schemes. It also enhances the revenue collection capacity, so as to safeguard the proper implementation of the budget. At the same time, it includes a programme of social rehabilitation, without risking financial gaps in the domestic front.

c. By virtue of the above, the government could demand a full-fledged participation in the quantitative easing (QE) policy, which is currently exercised by the ECB but still excludes Greece. Participation would allow a revitalization of Greek banks both by injecting liquidity and diminishing Grexit fears. By enhancing economic activity and liquidity, a lot more things may come under control and capital flight would subside. In turn, a full-scale negotiation would look feasible and justified.

At the time of completing this book, a nervous uncertainty continues to prevail in Athens and Brussels as to which course events may finally take. A clear and comprehensive strategy can lead to an orderly termination of the bailout programme and set off a period of rebuilding Greece's full-fledged participation in the Eurozone and the EU in general. In the absence of such a framework, Greece would be entangled in everlasting uncertainty and the chaos that a Grexit entails.

NOTES

1. FT Jan 22, 2015. http://www.ft.com/cms/s/0/639cf9b0-a1a0-11e4-bd03-00144feab7

2. CNBC http://www.cnbc.com/id/102367704, January 26, 2015.

3. The action was supported by the trade union of civil servants. See To Vima, 7 April 2015.

4. See the report e.g. in http://www.dailyforex.com/forex-fundamental-analysis

5 'EU frustration at Greece boils over'. *Financial Times*, 25 April 2015, p. 1.

Postscript

The writing of the book was completed as recently as April 2015, but time in Greece since then was running wild with the country verging on the brink of chaos and collapse. Negotiations between the left-wing Government and the lending institutions were always problematic, though a glimpse of hope emerged in June 22 when Greek proposals were for the first time taken as the basis of agreement. However, hardliners in the Euro Group demanded more measures and talks collapsed just a few days before the adjustment program was formally ended. The Greek Government unwisely chose to organize a referendum that was followed by bank panic. Within hours, heavy capital controls were imposed that sent banks to long holidays and the economy in tatters.

Amid accusations on the legality and meaning of the vote, the outcome was a heavy rejection of the proposals laid out by the lenders. The supporters of Grexit took it as the high opportunity to implement their plans, though the Prime Minister was quick enough to denounce them by claiming that the vote was no more than a helping tip on the negotiation table. The European leaders called his bluff and put the dilemma squarely on the Greek Government to choose between Grexit and a more extensive third memorandum with some pledges on investment financing to rekindle growth. After dramatic negotiations, a compromise was found at the dawn of July 13, and was subsequently voted by most parties in the Greek parliament. The Government, however, lost a quarter of its MPs and the dissenters formed a new group openly advocating Grexit. Unable to control the revolt, the Prime Minister resigned and an interim Government was formed with a mandate until the elections of 20, September 2015. (In the interim Government, the present author held the portfolio of Economic Development).

As the new program contains several fiscal measures, recession is likely to continue and this will make debt less sustainable and the political management less effective, no matter the election outcome. Thus the key questions put forward by the book remain wide open, albeit now both Greece and its European partners seem to be exhausted and frustrated more than ever. The dilemma between growth and Grexit is bound to be resolved sooner rather than later.

September 2015
Nicos Christodoulakis

Relevant Books and Research by the Author

RELEVANT BOOKS BY THE AUTHOR, PUBLISHED IN GREEK

B1. Christodoulakis N., 2014. Euro or Drachma? Dilemmas, illusions and vested interests. (Ευρώ ή Δραχμή? Διλήμματα Πλάνες και Συμφέροντα). Athens, Gutenberg Publications.

B2. Christodoulakis N., 2011. Can the Titanic be rescued? From the Austerity Memorandum, Back to Growth. (Σώζεται ο Τιτανικός; Από το Μνημόνιο ξανά στην Ανάπτυξη). Athens, Polis Publications.

RELEVANT RESEARCH BY THE AUTHOR

P1. 'Underinvestment and underemployment: the double hazard in the Euro Area', 2015. *Bank of Greece, Working Paper.*

P2. 'External imbalances in the Eurozone and the role of foreign direct investment', 2015. *The World Economy.* (Forthcoming). With V. Sarantides.

P3. 'Electoral misgovernance cycles: Tax evasion and wildfires in Greece', 2014. *Public Choice,* Vol. 159, 3–4, pp. 533–559, June. (With S. Skouras).

P4. 'Currency crisis and collapse in interwar Greece: Predicament or policy failure?', 2013a. *European Review of Economic History,* Vol. 17, 3, pp. 272–293.

P5. 'From Grexit to Growth: On fiscal multipliers and how to end recession in Greece', 2013b. *National Institute Economic Review,* Special Issue on Growth, 224, pp. 66–76, London, May.

P6. 'Greek Crisis in perspective: Origins, threats and ways-out', 2012, *New Palgrave Dictionary of Economics,* September. *http://www.dictionaryofeconomics.com/article?id=pde2012_G000221*

P7. 'Market reforms in Greece 1990–2008', 2012. In Kalyvas S. et al. (eds) *'From Stagnation to Forced Adjustment: Reforms in Greece, 1974–2010',* Columbia University Press.

P8. 'From indecision to fast-track privatizations: Can Greece still do it?', 2011. *National Institute Economic Review*, London, July.

P9. 'Crisis, Threats and Ways out for the Greek Economy', 2010. *Cyprus Economic Policy Review*, Vol. 4, 1.

P10. 'Fiscal developments in Greece 1980–1992: A critical review', 1994. *European Economy*, Vol. 3, pp. 97–134.

ACKNOWLEDGEMENT

The author acknowledges that the above research articles have been utilized to support the arguments described in the book as described below:

Chapter 1:   Draws from publications [P6], [P9] and [P10]
Chapter 2:   Draws from publications [P2] and [P8]
Chapter 4:   Draws from publication [P5]
Chapter 5:   Draws from publication [P5]
Chapter 7:   Draws from publication [P4]
Chapter 9:   Draws from publication [P1]
Chapter 10:   Draws from publications [P7] and [P10]
Chapter 11:   Draws from publication [P3]

References

Abad J. and J. H. Galante, 2011. 'Spanish Constitutional Reform What Is Seen and Not Seen'. *CEPS, Policy Briefs*, No. 253. Brussels, September. http://aei.pitt.edu/32483/1/PB_253_Abad_and_Hernandez_on_Spanish_constitutional_reform.pdf.

Akerlof G. and R. Shiller, 2009. *Animal Spirits:How Human Psychology Drives the Economy, and Why It Matters for Global Capitalism*. Princeton University Press.

Alesina A. and R. Perotti, 1997. 'Fiscal Adjustments in OECD Countries: Composition and Macroeconomic Effects'. *IMF Staff Papers*, 44(2), pp. 210–248.

Alesina A. and S. Ardagna, 1998. 'Tales of Fiscal Adjustment'. *Economic Policy*, 13(27): 489–585.

Aristophanes, *The Frogs*. Translation by B.B. Rogers.

Azariadis C., 2011. "To Euro or Not to Euro", http://www.Huffingtonpost.Com/Costas-Azariadis/To-Euro-Or-Not-To-Euro_B_1078692.html.

Baker V., 2011. "Ten Years After Economic Collapse, Argentina Is Still in Recovery". *The Guardian*, 14/12.

Bank of Greece, 1947. *Governor's Report for the Years 1941–1946* (in Greek).

Bank of Greece, 1978. *The First Fifty Years* (in Greek).

Bank of Greece, 2014. *The Chronicle of the Great Crisis: The Bank of Greece 2008–2013*. Athens: Bank of Greece (Centre of Culture, Research and Documentation).

Baum A., Cr. Checherita-Westphal and Ph. Rother, 2012. 'Debt and growth new evidence for the Euro Area'. *ECB Working Paper*, Series no. 1450, July.

Blanchard O. and D. Leigh, 2013. 'Growth Forecast Errors and Fiscal Multipliers'. *IMF Working Papers*, WP/13/1, January.

Blanchard O. and F. Giavazzi, 2002. 'Current Account Deficits in the Euro Area. The End of the Feldstein Horioka Puzzle?'. *MIT Working Paper*, Series no. 03–05, September.

Blanchard O., 2006. 'Current Account Deficits in Rich Countries'. *IMF* Mundell-Fleming Lecture, November.

Blustein P., 2005. *And the Money Kept Rolling In (And Out): Wall Street, the IMF, and the Bankrupting of Argentina*. New York: Public Affairs.

Bordo M.D. and H. Rockoff, 1996. 'The Gold Standard as a "Good Housekeeping Seal of Approval" ', *Journal of Economic History*, 56, 389–428, June.

Cassidy J., 2013. 'The Reinhart and Rogoff Controversy: A Summing Up'. *The New Yorker*, April 26. http://www.newyorker.com/news/john-cassidy/.

Cecchetti St., M. Mohanty and F. Zampolli, 2011. 'The real effects of debt'. *BIS Working Papers*, 352, Bank for International Settlements.

Chaloner J., A. Evans and M. Pragnell, 2014. NExit: *Assessing the Economic Impact of the Netherlands Leaving the European Union.* London: Capital Economics.

Checherita Cr. and Ph. Rother, 2010. 'The Impact of High and Growing Government Debt on Economic Growth. An Empirical Investigation for the Euro Area'. *ECB Working Paper*, Series no. 1237, August.

Christodoulaki O., 2001. 'Industrial Growth in Greece between the Wars: A New Perspective'. *European Review of Economic History*, 5(1): 61–89.

Cottarelli C. and L. Jaramillo, 2012. 'Walking Hand in Hand: Fiscal Policy and Growth in Advanced Economies'. *IMF Working Papers*, No. 137, May.

De Grauwe P., 2010. 'The Greek Crisis and the Future of the Eurozone'. *Intereconomics*, 2, pp. 89–93.

EC, 2009. *Quarterly Report on the Euro Area* 8(1). Brussels.

EC, 2012(a). GR 'Master Position Paper Main Messages Final Long Version: CF and ERDF 2014–2020'. *European Commission Services*, Internal Report. Brussels, 27 September.

EC, 2012(b). 'Position of the European Commission Services on the Development of Partnership Agreement and Programmes in Greece for the Period 2014–2020'. *European Commission*. Brussels, 13 November.

EC, 2012(c). 'The Second Economic Adjustment Programme for Greece: First Review'. *European Economy,* Occasional Papers 123. Brussels, December.

EC, 2013. 'The Second Economic Adjustment Programme for Greece: Second Review'. *European Economy*, Occasional Papers 148, May.

Eichengreen B. and J. Sachs, 1985. 'Exchange Rates and Economic Recovery in the 1930s'. *The Journal of Economic History*, 45(4), pp. 925–946. December.

Eichengreen B., 2012. 'When Currencies Collapse: Will We Replay the 1930s or the 1970s?'. *Foreign Affairs*, 91(1), 117–134. January/February.

European Commission, 2015. *European Economy, Vol. 2*. Economic Spring Forecast

ECB, 2001. *Monthly Bulletin*, September.

Feldstein M., 2012. 'The Failure of the Euro: The Little Currency That Couldn't'. *The Foreign Affairs*, January/February Issue.

Financial Times, 2015. 'EU Frustration at Greece Boils Over'. p. 1. 25 April.

Flood R. and Ch. Kramer, 1996. 'Economic Models of Speculative Attacks and the Drachma Crisis of May 1994'. *Open Economy Review*, 7, pp. 591–600.

Geithner T. 2014. *Stress Test: Reflections on Financial Crises*. New York: Crown Publishers.

Giavazzi F. and M. Pagano, 1990. 'Can Severe Fiscal Contractions Be Expansionary? Tales of Two Small European Countries'. *NBER Macroeconomics Annual*, 5, pp. 75–122. MIT Press.

Giavazzi F. and M. Pagano, 1996. 'Non-Keynesian Effects of Fiscal Policy Changes: International Evidence and the Swedish Experience'. *Swedish Economic Policy Review*, 3(1), pp. 67–103.

Gros D., 2015. 'The End of Fiscal Waterboarding?' *Centre for Economic Policy Studies, CEPS*. Brussels, 23 February. http://www.ceps.be/systcm/files/COMDG.

Hartwich, O.M., 2011. Unravelling the Greek Basket Case. *Business Spectator*, 20 Octobcr.

Herndon T., M. Ash and R. Pollin, 2013. 'Does High Public Debt Consistently Stifle Economic Growth? A Critique of Reinhart and Rogoff'. *Political Economy Research Institute*, University of Massachusetts, Amherst. Working Paper, Series no. 322. http://www.Businessspectator.Com.Au/Bs.Nsf/Article/Greece-Default-Eurozone-Monetary-Union-Soverieng-D-Pd20111017-Mq2gw?Opendocument&Src=Rss. http://www.foreignaffairs.com/articles/136752/martin-feldstein/the-failure-of-the-euro. http://www.dailyforex.com/forex-fundamental-analysis. http://www.theguardian.com/commentisfree/2011/dec/14/10-years-argentina-economic-collapse. http://blogs.ft.com/brusselsblog/2014/11/11/draghis-ecb-management-the-leaked-geithner-files/. http://www.bloomberg.com/markets/rates-bonds/government-bonds/germany. 23/1/2014.

Huntington S., 1993. 'The Clash of Civilizations?' *Foreign Affairs*, 72(3).

Jonung L. and E. Drea, 2009. 'The Euro: It Can't Happen. It's a Bad Idea. It Won't Last. US Economists on the EMU, 1989–2002'. *European Economy*, Economic Papers 395, December.

Keynes J.M., 1931. *Essays on Persuasion*. London: Macmillan.

Keynes J.M., 1936. *The General Theory of Employment, Interest and Money*. MacMillan Cambridge University Press (reprinted 1978).

Klein N., 2003. 'Out of the Ordinary'. *The Guardian*. [POnline] 25 January. http://www.guardian.co.uk/weekend/story/0,,880651,00.html.

Kolev A., T. Tanayama, and R. Wagenvoort, 2013. 'Investment and Investment Finance in Europe'. *European Investment Bank*, Economics Department.

Kopsidis M., 2012. 'Missed Opportunity or Inevitable Failure? The Search for Industrialization in Southeast Europe 1870–1940'. *European Historical Economics Society (EHES)*. Working Papers no. 19 July.

Kostis K., 1986. *Banks and the Crisis, 1929–1932*. Athens: Historical Archive, Commercial Bank of Greece (in Greek).

Krugman P., 2011. 'Origins of the Euro Crisis', blog *The Conscience of a Liberal*, 23 September.

Krugman, 2015. http://www.dailyforex.com/forex-fundamental-analysis.

Kumar, M.S. and J. Woo, 2010. 'Public Debt and Growth'. *IMF Working Papers*, 10/174.

Levy M. and P. Kretzmer, 2012. 'Greece's predicament: Lessons from Argentina'. 16 May. http://www.voxeu.org/article/greece-s-predicament-lessons-argentina.

Lustig N., L.F. Lopez-Calva and E. Ortiz-Juarez, 2012. 'Declining Inequality in Latin America in the 2000s: The Cases of Argentina, Brazil, and Mexico'. *The World Bank*, Policy Research Working Paper no. 6248, October.

Mabbett D. and W. Schelkle, 2010. 'Beyond the Crisis: the Greek Conundrum and EMU Reform'. *Intereconomics*, 2, pp. 81–85.

Maimoukas G., 1945. *Forty five Days of Economic Policy*. Athens: Self-edition (in Greek).

Mamatzakis Emm., 2014. 'Greek Statistics: Unraveling Ariadne's Thread Ball'. In Roukanas S.P. and P. Sklias (Eds), pp. 135–151. Athens: Livanis Publications (in Greek).

Mollenkamp C., 2010. 'London Firm Was Created to Route Cash', http://www.wsj.com/articles/SB10001424052748703791504575079903903971986. February 25.

OECD, 2013. Economic Surveys: Greece, November.

Papadopoulos Y., 2014. 'Olympic Desolation, Ten Years After', *Kathimerini (Daily)*. August 15 (in Greek).

Pisani-Ferry J., 2011. *Le réveil des démons: La crise de l'euro et comment nous en sortir*. Fayard.

Psalidopoulos M., 2011. 'Monetary Policy and Financial Crisis, 1929–1941'. *Bank of Greece*, July (in Greek).

Reinhart C.M. and K.S. Rogoff, 2010. 'Growth in a Time of Debt'. *American Economic Review*, 100(2), 573–578.

Roubini N., 2011. 'Greece Should Default, Leave the Euro and Reinstate the Drachma'. http://www.bloomberg.com/News/2011-09-19/Greece-Should-Default-Leave-Eurozone-Roubini-Writes-In-Ft.html.

Roukanas S.P. and P. Sklias (Eds), 2014. *Greek Political Economy 2000–2010: From EMU to the Bailout Mechanism*. Athens: Livanis Publishing Company.

Shearer, R. and C. Clark, 1984. 'Canada and the Interwar Gold Standard, 1920–1935: Monetary Policy without a Central Bank', In Bordo M. and A. Schwartz, (Eds), *Retrospective on The Classical Gold Standard, 1821–1931*, University of Chicago Press, http://www.nber.org/books/bord84-1.

Shelburne R.C., 2008. 'Current Account Deficits in European Emerging Markets'. *UN Discussion Paper*, no. 2008. 2 June.

Smith H., 2012. 'Athens 2004 Olympics: What Happened after the Athletes Went Home?' *The Guardian*, May 9. http://www.theguardian.com/sport/2012/may/09/athens-2004-olympics-athletes-home?

Spiegel P., 2014. http://blogs.ft.com/brusselsblog/2014/11/11/draghis-ecb-management-the-leaked-geithner-files/. *Financial Times*, November 2011.

Stiglitz J., 2002. *Globalization and Its Discontents*. London: Penguin Allen Lane.

Tsamadias C., 2014. The Growth Rate of the Economy, Public Deficit and Public Debt during the Post-dictatorship Period: A Comparative Assessment". In Roukanas S.P. and P. Sklias (Eds), pp. 96–134.

Vanatta S., 2012. 'History Offers an Ugly Precedent for a Greek Euro Exit', 1 June, http://www.bloomberg.com/news/2012-06-01/History-Offers-Ugly-Precedent-For-Greek-Euro-Exit.html.

Wandschneider K., 2008. 'The Stability of the Inter-War Gold Exchange Standard: Did Politics Matter?', *The Journal of Economic History*, 68(1), pp. 151–181.

WEO 2010. *Recovery, Risk and Rebalancing*. IMF, October.

WEO 2012. *Coping with High Debt and Sluggish Growth*. IMF, October.

Weisbrot M., 2011. 'Why Greece Should Reject the Euro', *New York Times*, Op-ed, 9 May. http://www.nytimes.com/2011/05/10/opinion/10weisbrot.html?_r=2

Williamson J., 1990. 'What Washington Means by Policy Reform'. Article in Williamson J. (Ed.) *Latin American Readjustment: How Much Has Happened*. Washington, Institute for International Economics.

Index